CAROLYN MOFFATT

INTRODUCTION TO HUMAN MOVEMENT

INTRODUCTION TO
HUMAN MOVEMENT

ADDISON-WESLEY PUBLISHING COMPANY

Edited by
HOPE M. SMITH
Purdue University

Contributing Authors

JANE A. MAVER
BARBARA J. MEAD
CAROLE A. OGLESBY
RAY ANNE SHRADER
CAROL J. WIDULE

Reading, Massachusetts · Menlo Park, California · London · Don Mills, Ontario

This book is in the
Addison-Wesley Series in Physical Education

FOREWORD

Courage to take a new direction in any endeavor requires a combination of vision, new knowledge, experience, and innovative spirit. In recent years some physical educators have, despite tradition, sought to identify the phenomena of man's behavior, which should rightfully be within their area of study. They are committed to the importance of studying the human in motion.

In 1964 the Department of Physical Education for Women at Purdue University identified the study of human movement as the major focus for guiding the development of entirely new programs and curricula for all levels. The many hours of faculty thought, study, research, and discussion which ensued are perhaps best summarized by products which colleagues in the field can view. With several projects underway and some already completed, the department welcomes this opportunity to share with interested colleagues and students what it considers to be an introduction to the study of human movement.

A description of the nature and contents of this book is best left to the editor. However, the process which led to the publication of this book should be described.

A general theoretical framework, initially developed for establishing a new graduate program at Purdue University, became the basis of an idea for a course in physical activity for all freshmen women. Subsequently, a small group of faculty volunteers worked together to identify potential areas for study within this theoretical framework. Specific concepts and subconcepts evolved from the continuing dedication of the faculty to analysis of available facts concerning the human in motion. Paralleling this investigation was another: the faculty sought information about the physical education experiences of freshmen women prior to their enrollment at the university. Information from this source aided in selecting the level of conceptual material to be included in a two semester, one-year course. It was the purpose of this proposed course to introduce all students to the major areas of study in the field of human movement.

Eventual organization of the course, Introduction to Human Movement, included the presentation of conceptual information in a logical sequence for study. In order to be conducted on an experimental basis for one year, this new course required the preparation of written materials for student use. Materials were unavailable for some areas of human movement, for example, perception, aesthetics, and socio-cultural phenomena. Other conceptual information was found in the physical education literature and in the literature of related disciplines, but the broader connotations and the applications to the movement behavior of individuals (apart from the purposes for which the individual moves) were noticeably lacking. Therefore, appropriate materials for students were developed by the faculty. While some of this information is not new, the perspective from which this material is discussed provides the reader with a broader view than has been presented before.

A preliminary edition of some of the materials contained in this book was made available by the publisher for exclusive use of the Purdue faculty and students. Appraisal by students, faculty, and colleagues in the field indicated that this book could serve not only the course for which it was designed, but, with revision, it might become a source for those studying and working in many areas of physical education. Subsequently, a reorganization of the material in the preliminary edition was made and additional information was identified for inclusion in this present publication.

As the various phenomena of human movement receive increasing attention and study by scholars in our field, undoubtedly many books of this nature will appear. This particular book is timely, however, in that it symbolizes a faculty commitment to a focus of study that sharply departs from the traditional ideas of physical education. The faculty is to be commended for its dedication to a conceptual scheme, for its flexibility in thinking, and for its courage in innovation. The freedom of the department to assume a nontraditional focus of study was made possible, however, only through the understanding and support of the administration. For this we are indeed grateful to Purdue University.

Marguerite A. Clifton, Head
Department of
Physical Education for Women

PREFACE

Most of us know exactly what "physical education" means because we experienced it during most of our school years. To some of us it was a period of the school day when we changed our clothes, donned "gym suits" and "sneakers" or "tennis shoes," and went into the gym or out on the fields to play various games and sports. Some of us enjoyed these periods of release from sitting in the classroom and others did not because we met with little success in the kinds of activities we experienced. We equated the physical education class either with "release from tension" and "letting off steam" or with playing games that we did or did not enjoy depending on the sport season and the level of skillfulness we achieved in the various phases of the activity.

Only in rare instances did we leave twelve years of physical education behind us knowing much more about our motor performance except that we play some games well enough to engage in them occasionally and that we play others poorly or not at all. We may know that regular, vigorous exercise and "fitness" are closely related, but since we seem to get along without the exercise, why should we worry? Consider, then, all the things we have not learned about physical activity, for example, very few of us know that certain ways of approaching the learning of a new activity, or the refining of a familiar activity, are far more effective than others; that selecting certain sensory information to attend to is important for improving performance; that the design of the human body is such that it permits an enormous number of movements and movement combinations; that the physical environment in which we live imposes certain restrictions on our movement behavior (if the laws of that environment and the operational principles derived from these laws are understood and applied, one may move efficiently despite the restrictions); that our socio-cultural environment affects the ways in which we use space-time with our bodies and body segments and that our environment influences the value we assign to various activities and our ability to perform them.

Since the reader usually has preconceived notions about physical education, it will be necessary for him to reorganize his perceptual framework so that he views the materials presented in this book from a new perspective. The reader should not expect a detailed description of skill progressions in a variety of sports and games, nor a digest of sports rules, nor a number of simplified guides to better bowling, swimming, or dancing. This kind of information may be found in other texts.

Rather he should approach his reading with the expectation of learning about movement as a phenomenon, about the forces and human variables that shape it, and about the principles to be applied in refining his own movement behavior, whether he moves for recreation, work production, survival, or the development and maintenance of health.

Lafayette, Indiana   H. M. S.
February 1968

ACKNOWLEDGMENTS

The production of this book is dependent on the work and cooperation of a great many people whose contributions cannot be individually recognized in the completed volume. Therefore, the authors wish to thank, first of all, their colleagues in the Department of Physical Education for Women, Purdue University, who read the preliminary edition and gave many constructive suggestions for additions and deletions which were acted upon in the final draft. The authors are also grateful for the evaluations of the preliminary edition by the 1500 freshman women of Purdue who used these materials as a text in their course, Introduction To Human Movement, during the 1966–67 academic year.

To those professional colleagues who reviewed the final manuscript at the request of the publishers, the authors are indeed grateful. Their critiques were thorough and thoughtful, and many of their suggestions have been incorporated in this publication.

Special acknowledgment must be given to Mrs. Logan Wright, a former member of the Purdue staff, who collated some of the materials which appeared in the preliminary edition. Due to editorial and format changes, these contributions do not appear in the final manuscript, but we are indebted to Patsy for allowing us to use her materials during the "dry run" period.

The authors (particularly the editor) are most appreciative of the work of Mrs. Robert Weisbach who translated a tremendous amount of bad handwriting and editorial scribbling into clean, readable, typed copy and even managed to meet impossible deadlines for the preliminary edition and final manuscript.

Though publishers are rarely mentioned in acknowledgments by authors, we, however, offer a special vote of thanks to Addison-Wesley, in particular to their representatives for their constant encouragement and their belief and assistance in sponsoring a project that departs considerably from the mainstream of physical education literature.

CONTENTS

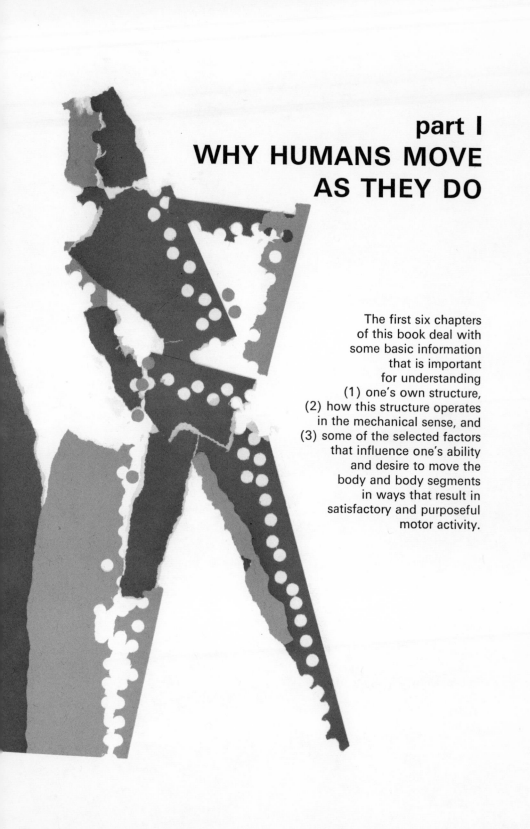

part I
WHY HUMANS MOVE
AS THEY DO

The first six chapters
of this book deal with
some basic information
that is important
for understanding
(1) one's own structure,
(2) how this structure operates
in the mechanical sense, and
(3) some of the selected factors
that influence one's ability
and desire to move the
body and body segments
in ways that result in
satisfactory and purposeful
motor activity.

chapter 1

THE NATURE OF
HUMAN MOVEMENT

One of the most complex of all phenomena associated with that most complex of living organisms—the human being—is the way in which he moves through his environment. If we view this process of movement in the abstract, without considering purpose, we may define it as the change of position of the body or body segments in space and time through the application of varying degrees of force.

Now this seems a rather easy way to dismiss the topic—with a tidy, uncomplicated definition. But the complexities of the subject are not explained by a mere definition. And even if they were, the topic could not be dismissed, for the simple reason that movement is a basic ingredient of all one's life and living.

Movement of the growing organism is one of the first signs of new life; it has been detected as early as the embryonic stage of development *in utero* and has been even more clearly identified in the fetal stage of growth. Man's equation of the term "movement" with life itself is reflected, at least in the English language, by the use of the word "stillborn"—"still" being the antonym for "moving"—to denote the absence of life in a newborn child.

The orderly patterns of growth in the healthy young baby are signaled by his increasing ability to move through space. One of the proudest moments in a parent's life is the moment when baby takes his first steps, for this is evidence that the child is progressing normally in his acquisition of abilities that are characteristic of the human species.

BIPEDALISM AND HUMAN EVOLUTION

Of all the animals, man has been the most successful in the constant struggle with his environment. Even though he cannot run as fast as the quadripeds, swim as well as the dolphin, climb as well as the apes, or fly as birds do, he

3

has been the only creature able to defy the force of gravity and move into outer space. One underlying factor that has enabled man to accomplish this feat is his ability to move through the environment on two legs. As he has progressed on the evolutionary scale since the Australopithecine Stage, during which the earliest evidence of consistent bipedal locomotion has been found, man has walked in an upright position. With his two hands freed to experiment with the physical materials of his world, and by virtue of the unique advantage of the opposable thumb, he has become a fashioner of tools, a manipulator of his environment, an explorer and creator. According to some anthropologists, it is this fact, coupled with the eventual pressures of natural selection, that has led to the increase in the size and complexity of his brain.

But why is it that man can walk on two legs, while the dog, the horse, or the sheep must walk on four? The explanation lies in one specialized part of man's skeletal structure that sets him apart from all other mammals: the ilium, or hip bone. This is a broad, flat bone into which the head of the femur (thigh bone) is set. The two ilia form, with other bony processes, the pelvic girdle. It is the peculiar and specialized shape of these bones and the musculature of the hips that enables man to achieve bipedal locomotion as a consistent way of moving through the environment.

Although man has built machines to move him from place to place at ever-faster rates, these technological advances have caused little if any change in his structure from what it was 40,000 years ago.* His chief means of locomotion is still his two legs, even if it is only to walk to and from his automobile or airplane. In an automated society such as our own, the ability to do work and to travel with less and less physical effort for the individual has resulted in many benefits. Unfortunately, there are certain "side-effects" that have *not* been to our advantage. Among them are the so-called hypokinetic diseases. These are malfunctions of the human organism caused, in great measure, by a lack of regular, vigorous physical activity. In short, our 40,000-year-old structures have not yet adapted, through mutation and natural selection processes, to our twentieth-century technology.

THE STRUGGLE AGAINST GRAVITY

From the moment we are born the struggle against gravity begins. As we progress through the age-old developmental patterns, i.e., the movement of the head, waving and flexing of the arms, kicking of the legs, attempting to sit upright, creeping, crawling, and eventually walking, we engage in a never-ending contest against gravitational force.

* See Sol Tax (ed.), *The Evolution of Man: Man, Culture and Society*, Vol. II. Chicago: The University of Chicago Press, 1960.

We experiment throughout life, each of us an unsung Newton, with the laws and principles of our physical environment. Although our structures enable us to move in many ways, the physical laws place certain restrictions on us. For example, we soon learn, as we take the first tentative steps, that "what goes up must come down"! Some of us learn to enjoy the struggle tremendously and persist until we have run faster, jumped farther, leaped higher, or twirled faster than anyone ever has before us. Thus a Wilma Rudolph, a Ralph Boston, a Valery Brumel (Olympic gold medalists), a Peggy Fleming (champion figure skater), and a Rudolph Nureyev (noted ballet dancer) are made. True, while the athletes and dancers are achieving greater successes in this constant struggle, most of us are lucky to be able to walk with some semblance of poise, run fast enough to catch the bus, jump far enough to avoid landing in a mud puddle, or do the latest dance step before it goes out of style. Yet success in performing each one of these mundane activities is dependent on how well we have learned to move our structures within the limits imposed by the physical laws that govern motion in the earth's atmosphere.

STYLES OF MOVEMENT BEHAVIOR

All human beings everywhere, if they are not handicapped by disease or injury, move in basically the same way. But from individual to individual there are subtle differences in styles of moving that present an infinite number of variations on a theme. Each of us, as he gains the ability to maintain equilibrium while in an upright position and explores the environment by moving through it, develops his own unique and characteristic movement behavior. The manner in which we walk becomes almost as unmistakable an identification mark as our fingerprints. As a matter of fact, we very often distinguish one friend or acquaintance from another by the differences in their walking gaits and characteristic postures.

Many factors are involved in the formation of one's movement behavior. Let's examine your own. The very first influence, of course, is the set of parents you happened to choose. You have inherited from them, as they did from your grandparents, a particular body type which may or may not facilitate your moving efficiently in a variety of ways. You have also inherited an organic system, a metabolic rate, and a nervous system that all have some effect on the quality with which you move. In addition, your movement behavior is, of course, influenced by the environment into which you were born—not just the physical environment of earth and the geographical location, but your family, your neighborhood, and many other social-cultural factors. Your unique movement behavior is thus a product of an interaction between the "inherited you" and your physical-social environment.

MOVEMENT AND PURPOSE

Almost all movement is purposeful. We say "almost" because under some medically abnormal conditions involuntary, nonpurposeful motor responses may be evidenced. Some purposes are immediate and identifiable, while others are long-range and not at all apparent to anyone but the mover himself.

For example, we observe a friend performing the forehand drive in tennis. Her immediate and obvious purpose for moving in specific ways is to drive the ball across the net into some part of her opponent's court. But her long-range purpose is not apparent to us. She may be hoping to perfect her game for social reasons (her boyfriend has asked her to play in the mixed-doubles tournament with him), or perhaps she is intent on learning to play well enough so that she can eventually get some enjoyable and vigorous exercise. On the other hand, she may be refining her skill for the sheer aesthetic pleasure she gets from hitting the tennis ball speedily, accurately, and consistently. Her long-range purpose could be all of these, any one of these, or none of these. One thing, we can be sure of, however, is that she is engaged in purposeful motion—even if the purposes we assign to her and her own long-range goals do not happen to coincide.

At the beginning of life, movement occurs simply as a motor response to one's internal and external environmental stimuli. The baby's "purposes" in moving are to avoid pain, satisfy hunger, etc. But as the infant grows into child, adolescent, and adult, he acquires many more purposes for motion— to satisfy curiosity, to develop natural abilities, to obtain necessities or gratify tastes, to express and communicate ideas, emotions, and information—the list is endless. Some movement patterns are employed for purely survival purposes, while others serve in play, recreation, and release from stress and tension. One must move in myriad ways to perform the daily tasks involved in caring for self and family. There are buttons to be buttoned, shoes to be tied, clothes to be ironed, mouths to be fed, beds to be made, rugs to be vacuumed, and a thousand-and-one other chores to be done, and they all require that we move ourselves and other physical bodies through space. Last, but certainly not the least important, in our list of general purposes for moving through space is the development and maintenance of a healthy, well-functioning, aesthetically pleasing body. There is much evidence that regular, vigorous physical activity, along with a balanced diet and adequate rest, is a major factor in the maintenance of total fitness for living and the enjoyment of living.

SUMMARY

1. Human movement may be defined as the change of position of the body or body parts in space and time.
2. Movement of growing organisms is one of the first signs of life.
3. One of the two basic factors that dictate the characteristics of human movement is human structure, which has evidenced little change in the last 40,000 years. The other basic determinant is gravity, together with the whole body of laws pertaining to motion in the earth's atmosphere.
4. Although movement is fundamentally the same throughout the human species, there are individual variations or styles of moving. The term "movement behavior" is used to denote any individual's unique and characteristic ways of moving. Differences in movement behavior are the result of many influences. These include: (1) heredity, (2) geographic location, and (3) social-cultural values and expectations.
5. Almost all movement behavior is purposeful. Some general purposes are: (1) survival, (2) satisfaction of curiosity, (3) development of abilities, (4) communication, including the expression of ideas and feelings, (5) recreation, play, and release from tension, (6) the performance of daily tasks, and (7) the development and maintenance of fitness.

SUGGESTED READING

GESELL, ARNOLD, et al., *The First Five Years of Life.* New York: Harper & Row, 1940

HUIZINGA, JOHAN, *Homo Ludens.* Boston: The Beacon Press, 1955

METHENY, ELEANOR, "The unique meaning inherent in human movement," *The Physical Educator* 18, 3–7 (1961)

SMITH, HOPE, AND MARGUERITE CLIFTON, *Physical Education: Exploring Your Future.* Englewood Cliffs, N.J.: Prentice-Hall, Inc., 1962 (Chapter I, pp. 7–9, "Movement — A Common Factor")

TAX, SOL (ed.), *The Evolution of Man: Man, Culture and Society,* Vol. II. Chicago: The University of Chicago Press, 1960

chapter 2
BIOLOGICAL BASES OF
HUMAN MOVEMENT

In the previous chapter we noted that the human being moves through his environment in specific ways because of his unique structure. From birth, the child engages in an orderly sequence of movement experiences. Through the process of maturation he acquires many complex patterns of movement behavior, and—although movement is fundamentally the same in the human species—he acquires his own unique and characteristic ways of moving. In this chapter, we shall identify some of the biological mechanisms that underlie this capacity of the human organism to move and to adapt to his environment.

TISSUES OF THE BODY

A tissue is "a group of two or more cells having a similar combined function."* The function of one body tissue must be integrated with that of other body tissues if the body is to maintain the constancy that is required for health and welfare. The integration and regulation of function of the body tissues becomes particularly important when the physiological systems of the body are required to adapt to the demands imposed by vigorous physical activity. Body tissues are considered first here in terms of their specific structure and function, and then in terms of their role in the function of various organs and organ systems of the body, particularly as they are affected by movement activities.

---

* Harold W. Manner, *Elements of Anatomy and Physiology*. Philadelphia: W. B. Saunders Company, 1964.

Connective Tissue

As the name implies, the function of connective tissue is to connect other tissues of the body. Two types of fibers are found in connective tissue. *Collagenous* fibers are characterized by their inelasticity and by their great strength. *Elastic* fibers are thinner than collagenous fibers and possess the property of elasticity. *Tendons,* a form of connective tissue composed primarily of collagenous fibers, connect muscle to bone, and function to transfer muscular contractions across the articulation of the joints. *Ligaments,* by contrast, unite bone to bone. Most ligaments are composed of collagenous fibers, but a few are composed almost entirely of elastic fibers. This is especially true of ligaments connecting the posterior surfaces of the spinal column.*

Bone is the hardest of the connective tissues and forms most of the skeletal structure of the adult human body. The bones serve primarily as support and protection for the soft tissues and vital organs of the body and as a framework for the attachment of muscles. Bones are covered by a dense, fibrous connective tissue called the *periosteum.* This membrane is usually firmly united to the bony tissues, which in turn combine with collagenous fibers in the bone. The tendons of muscles insert into the periosteum.

Muscle Tissue

The function of muscle tissue is to exert force on body parts by contraction. *Skeletal muscles* are attached to bones by tendons, and the contraction of these muscles results in a displacement of the body or body segments. The contraction of *cardiac muscle* controls the pumping of blood, while the contraction of *smooth muscle* affects digestion, circulation, and other internal functions of the body. The discussion in this chapter is related primarily to skeletal muscle tissue because of the importance of skeletal muscle activity to bodily movement.

Skeletal muscle is composed of many fibers, each bounded by connective tissue. Each fiber, in turn, consists of many bundles of closely packed *fibrils.* The fibrils are made up of two types of filaments that give to skeletal muscles their characteristic striated appearance (see Fig. 2–1). Although the exact mechanism of muscular contraction is still not completely understood, electron microscope studies have established that contraction does involve an interaction between these two types of filaments in the muscle fibrils.

The contractions of skeletal muscles have been classified according to the apparent amount and direction of the displacement of body segments. For example, in *concentric contraction,* as the muscle shortens the body segment

* See W. Henry Hollinshead, *Functional Anatomy of the Limbs and Body.* Philadelphia: W. B. Saunders Company, 1960.

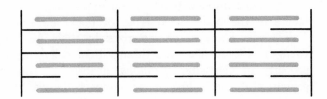

Fig. 2–1. Schematic arrangement of the two types of filaments in the muscle fibril.

is displaced in the direction of the muscle's line of pull. The adjective *isotonic*, which means "of equal tension," is commonly used in connection with concentric contraction. In fact, however, in concentric contraction the tension in the muscle does not necessarily remain the same. The term merely indicates that the muscle has decreased in length.

The term *eccentric contraction* indicates a gradual releasing of the tension in a muscle as it gives in to gravity or to some other force greater than that of the contracting muscle. As the muscle gradually releases tension it returns to its normal resting length.

When the muscle remains in partial or complete contraction with no apparent displacement of body segments, it is said to be in *static contraction*. This may occur when muscles that are antagonistic to each other contract with equal strength, when one is holding or supporting an object against another force such as the pull of gravity, or when one is attempting to move an object that presents greater resistance than the muscle is capable of overcoming. The term *isometric*, which means "of equal length," is used synonymously with static contraction when muscle tension is maximum.

Gradations of muscular contraction depend on neurological, physiological, and environmental factors. Some of these factors are considered later in this chapter and a more detailed discussion is included in Chapter 8 in reference to the strength and endurance of skeletal muscles.

Nervous Tissue

Nerves are tissues specialized for conduction and whose combined functioning serves to coordinate all aspects of human behavior. Through the various specialized parts of the nervous system, the body is able to adjust to changes in both the internal and the external environments.

The basic unit of the nervous system is the *neuron*, which is composed of three parts: the *cell body, dendrites* (which carry impulses toward the

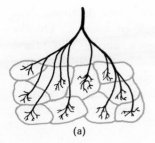 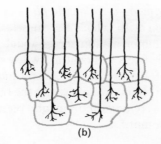

(a)   (b)

Fig. 2–2. Schematic diagram of neuromuscular relationships. In (a), one motor nerve innervates ten muscle fibers. In (b), each motor nerve innervates only one muscle fiber. The ratio of motor nerves to muscle fibers depends on the function of the muscle.

nerve cell body), and an *axon* (which carries impulses away from the nerve cell body). All bodily movements depend on the integrative action of two types of nerve fibers. *Sensory* (or *afferent*) fibers conduct impulses from the periphery of the body to the central nervous system. *Motor* (or *efferent*) fibers conduct impulses from the central nervous system to the periphery.

The dendrites of the sensory neurons are specialized to receive stimuli, and terminate in *receptor end organs,* which are of three general types. *Exteroceptors,* end organs located at or near the body's surface, respond to conditions in the external environment. The receptors in the retina of the eye, which respond to light, are examples of this type of specialized end organ. *Interoceptors* enable us to be aware of various conditions in the internal environment. Some of the interoceptors respond to visceral sensations, for example, pain, hunger and thirst. A third type of receptor, *proprioceptors,* is found in the muscles, tendons, and joints, as well as in the labyrinth of the inner ear. While some of the proprioceptors provide us with information concerning the location of our bodies in space, others function only at a reflex level (that is, below the level of conscious awareness) in the regulation of posture and movement.

The axons of motor neurons may be quite long, for they extend from the central nervous system to the skeletal muscles. Just beyond the point where each axon enters a muscle, it divides into a number of secondary branches. Each of these branches terminates on the surface of a single muscle fiber, where it forms a specialized ending known as the *motor end plate.* A single motor neuron may serve a few or many muscle fibers. All muscle fibers served by the neuron will respond when stimulated by a nerve impulse; they are therefore considered as constituting one functional unit of the neuromuscular system. This unit is called a *motor unit* (see Fig. 2–2).

The *number of motor units* brought into play for a particular muscle determines the strength of the contraction in that muscle (see Chapter 8);

the *ratio of motor neurons to muscle fibers* in each motor unit determines the degree of precision with which the muscle is capable of moving. On the average, a single motor neuron serves about 150 muscle fibers. This means that all 150 muscle fibers will contract when stimulated by the motor neuron. In the muscles of the eye, however, one motor neuron has been found to serve no more than 10 muscle fibers. At the other end of the scale are muscles that exhibit only very gross movements; these have as many as 200 or more fibers to the motor unit.*

Blood

The transport function of blood is important to the operation of every physiological system in the body. The cells of the blood include *red cells* (erythrocytes) and *white cells* (leukocytes). The red color of the erythrocytes is due to the presence of hemoglobin, which possesses the special property of readily taking up oxygen and also readily releasing the oxygen under certain circumstances. The red cells serve, therefore, for the transport of oxygen from the lungs to the other tissues of the body. The so-called white cells of the blood, which are actually rather transparent and colorless, function in several ways to protect the body against infection.

FUNCTIONING OF THE MUSCULO-SKELETAL SYSTEM

Joints

A joint is a union between one bone and another. Joints in the human body range from unions permitting no movement to those permitting very free movement.

The terms currently used to describe the actions of joints are not completely satisfactory. For one thing their usage with reference to some areas of the body is not consistent with the definitions. Another limitation is in the definitions themselves, for these assume that the movement starts with the body in the anatomical position (body straight, arms by the sides, palms facing forward) and that at the end of the movement the body has returned to the same position. Joint-action terms and definitions also differ from one text to another. There has been a recent attempt to standardize the terms and remove the ambiguities of joint-motion nomenclature but as yet this effort has not had widespread effect on usage.† Therefore, we present here

---

* See Arthur C. Guyton, *Function of the Human Body*. Philadelphia: W. B. Saunders Company, 1965.
† See J. A. Roebuck, Jr., "Kinesiology in engineering." Paper presented at the American Association for Health, Physical Education and Recreation Convention, Chicago, Illinois, March, 1966.

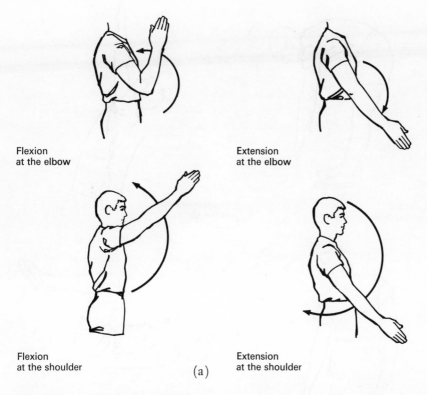

Flexion
at the elbow

Extension
at the elbow

Flexion
at the shoulder

Extension
at the shoulder

(a)

Fig. 2–3. Action at selected joints.

just a few of the frequently used joint-action terms, together with definitions that seem to be most consistent with general usage. Examples of the actions described are illustrated in Fig. 2–3 (a, b, c).

Flexion. Movement that decreases the angle formed at a joint.

Extension. The opposite of flexion: A body segment returns to its original anatomical position and the angle at the joint is increased.

Abduction. A body segment is moved laterally away from the longitudinal midline of the body.

Adduction. The opposite of abduction: A body segment returns to its original anatomical position by movement laterally toward the longitudinal midline of the body.

Rotation. Movement of a segment around its own longitudinal axis.

Circumduction. A body segment circumscribes a conical area or space.

Since movement of the body and body segments occurs as a result of action at the joints, the joint structure determines the kinds of movement

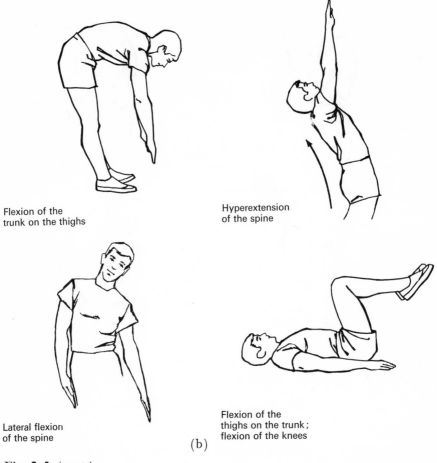

Flexion of the
trunk on the thighs

Hyperextension
of the spine

Lateral flexion
of the spine

Flexion of the
thighs on the trunk;
flexion of the knees

(b)

Fig. 2–3 (*cont.*).

that are possible. Two types of freely movable joints and their actions are described below, to illustrate some of the movement possibilities in the body.

1. A *hinge joint* permits movement in one plane only. The actions possible in hinge joints are flexion and extension. Examples are the joints of the knee, the elbow, and the fingers.

2. A *ball-and-socket joint*, as the name implies, is formed by the rounded head of one bone that fits into a cup-like structure of another bone. Joints of this type are the most freely movable joints in the body. Their structure allows for a wide variety of actions, including flexion, extension, abduction, adduction, and circumduction, as well as combinations of these basic actions. The ilio-femoral joint at the hip and the gleno-humeral joint at the shoulder are ball-and-socket joints.

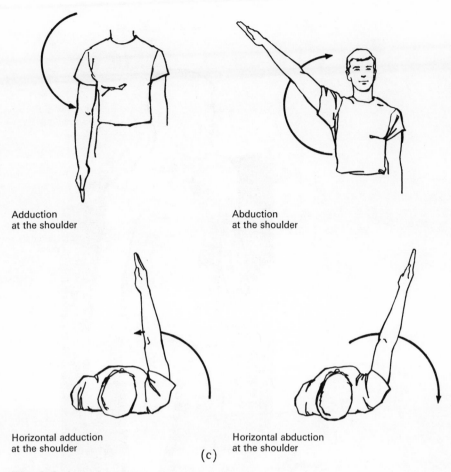

Adduction
at the shoulder

Abduction
at the shoulder

Horizontal adduction
at the shoulder

(c)

Horizontal abduction
at the shoulder

Fig. 2–3 (cont.).

Planes of Joint Motion

Movement of the body can be described in terms of the plane in which the action of the joint occurs (see Fig. 2–4). Assuming that when the movement occurs the body is in the anatomical position, flexion and extension occur in the *sagittal* plane. This is a plane that divides the body into a right-hand portion and a left-hand portion. Abduction and adduction occur in the *frontal* (or coronal) plane. This is a plane that divides the body into a front portion (anterior) and a back portion (posterior). Rotations occur in the *transverse* plane, which divides the body into an upper (superior) portion and a lower (inferior) portion. The three planes are at right angles to each other, and if these planes happen to intersect at the center of gravity of the body (see Chapter 3) they are identified as the *cardinal* sagittal, frontal, and transverse planes.

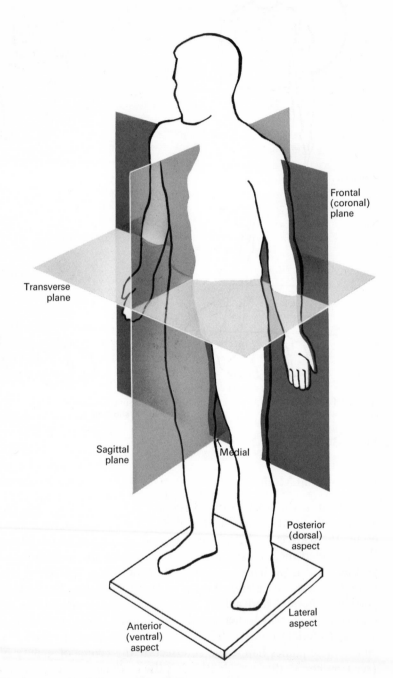

Fig. 2–4. The three cardinal planes of the body.

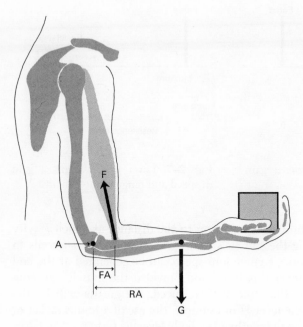

Fig. 2–5. Lever function of the musculo-skeletal system. *F*, line of action of the force; *G*, line of action of the resistance (the point at which gravity acts on the segment); *A*, the fulcrum (the axis of rotation); *FA*, the force arm (only approximate in this illustration, since the muscle is not pulling exactly at right angles to the bony lever); *RA*, resistance arm of the lever.

Body Levers

The bones of the body, articulated at joints, combine with the muscles that move them to form a system of levers. In physics, lever is defined as a rigid bar that turns about a fixed point called the *fulcrum*. In the body the bones are the rigid bars, the fulcrum is at the joint, and the turning action is supplied by muscular contraction. (See Fig. 2–5.) The function of a lever is to provide a mechanical advantage—either by amplifying the power of an applied force or by increasing the range and speed of movement. The particular advantage provided by any lever depends on the location of the fulcrum and the points at which the forces are acting on the rigid bar. A lever that has a long force arm and a short resistance arm favors a gain in force. A lever with a short force arm and a long resistance arm favors a gain in speed (see Figs. 2–6 and 2–7).

In the human body, the mechanical advantage that is gained in the movement of body segments generally tends to favor speed and range of movement. The distance between the fulcrum and the point of attachment of the muscle

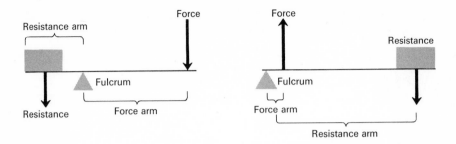

Fig. 2–6. Lever which favors a gain in power.

Fig. 2–7. Lever which favors a gain in speed and range of movement.

on the bone tends to be short in comparison to the distance at which gravity or other forces are resisting the muscle's pull. Once the muscle succeeds in overcoming the resisting force, tremendous speed can be generated at the end of the bony lever. The longer this lever, and provided the muscle can continue to move the lever at the same angular speed, the greater will be the linear speed at the end of the lever. For example, the use of a tennis racket or other implement enables one to lengthen the body leverage system.

It is important to note that the potential power that the muscle is capable of exerting on the bone is modified as the position of the segments in relation to each other is altered at the joint. The actual turning effect of the muscle on the bone is constantly changing. When the muscle is pulling at right angles to the bone it exerts maximum turning effect for a given amount of muscle tension. At other positions, the muscle must exert greater tension in order to maintain the same angular speed of movement (see Fig. 2–8).

CELLULAR RESPIRATION AND METABOLIC FUNCTIONS

The term *respiration* is usually used to refer to the exchange of oxygen and carbon dioxide between the cells of the body and the outside environment. But biologists also use the term for the biochemical events that occur inside living cells in the breakdown of food molecules and the transfer of the resulting energy to other molecules. This latter function may be more precisely referred to as cellular respiration. Food molecules can be stored within the body, but in man, oxygen cannot be stored, nor can carbon dioxide be allowed to accumulate for later disposal; therefore, respiratory gas exchange is a crucial and continuous process. On the other hand, the ability to engage in prolonged vigorous activity depends primarily on cellular respiratory adjustments.

The energy for engaging in any activity is derived in the first place from the oxidation of foodstuffs. This energy is then converted to electrical, mechanical, or thermal energy to drive biological reactions such as that

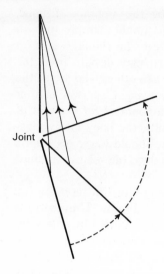

Joint

Fig. 2–8. The relationship of the joint position to the turning effect of the muscle. If the tension of the muscle remains constant, the turning effect is maximum when the muscle is acting at right angles to the bone.

required in muscular contraction. The name given to this total process is *metabolism*. In general, metabolic rates reflect the level of activity of the individual.

Whatever transformations it may undergo, eventually energy appears as heat. This means that total energy expenditure can be expressed in terms of its heat equivalent. In relation to biological processes, the *calorie* is used as a measure of energy. A calorie is the amount of heat required to raise the temperature of one kilogram of water one degree centigrade.

The amount of energy used for an activity can be found *directly*, by measuring the amount of heat produced, or *indirectly*, by calculating it from the amounts of oxygen absorbed and carbon dioxide eliminated. The oxygen consumption for moderate activity is equal to about 240 calories per hour, and an individual continuing at such a rate for an eight-hour day would use about 3800 calories. The oxygen consumption for *vigorous activity* is equal to about 360 calories an hour, and an individual continuing at such a rate for an eight-hour day would use about 4300 calories.*

Regulation of Body Weight

Body weight is a reflection of the balance between food intake and food utilization. An increase in body weight occurs when there is an excess of food

---

* See Ralph W. Stacy and John A. Santolucito, *Modern College Physiology*. St. Louis: The C. V. Mosby Company, 1966.

intake over utilization; the excess food is converted into fat and stored in adipose tissue.

Total body weight is determined primarily by the amount of bone, muscle, and fat in the body. The term *overweight* implies simply that an individual weighs more than published tables indicate he should weigh in relation to height, age, and sex. Such an individual may deviate from the average simply because he has a larger muscle mass than others who are of the same height, age, and sex. Thus the so-called "overweight" person may or may not be obese. In an obese person the relative amount of *fat* per unit of body weight is *greater* than normal. (In young adults, the body fat averages about 15% of the body weight.) If one is obese he should lower his calorie intake and increase his physical activity, and thus reduce the relative amount of fat contributing to his total body weight.

Experimentally, the body fat content can be determined in several ways. The whole-body liquid scintillation counter, used at Purdue University, is one such method. This technique measures gamma rays emitted by potassium in the body. Since potassium is associated with the lean body mass of the body, the lean body mass can be estimated, and then the fat content can be estimated by the difference between the lean body mass and the total body weight.* Body fat content can also be determined by measuring the density of the body, as for example by weighing the individual in air and again in water and applying Archimedes' principle (see Chapter 3). Another method depends on measurement of the thickness of skin folds.

Because bone structure remains relatively constant for the mature individual, the proportion of muscle and fat will determine to some extent whether weight is gained or lost as a result of exercise. Within certain limits, weight due to muscle is desirable because muscle is the contractile element that controls all movement possibilities. But similarly, a certain amount of body weight due to fat is necessary for health, for it represents reserve energy, it serves as insulation in cold weather, and it protects certain internal organs from injury. An excess of fat, however, not only represents an extra load that the individual is required to carry, but also places a strain on the circulatory system. It has been estimated that one pound of fat adds about one mile of additional small blood vessels to the circulatory system.

The storage and loss of fat depends on energy that is conserved in relation to energy that is expended. And since energy is measured in terms of calories, whether an individual gains or loses fat depends on the ratio of caloric intake (through food) to caloric output (through work) (see Fig. 2–9). If diet is held constant (or reduced), an increase in any form of physical activity increases energy expenditure and so will serve to take off

---

* See John E. Christian, Loyal W. Coombs, and Wayne V. Kessler, "The body composition of obese subjects." *American Journal of Clinical Nutrition* 15, 20–28 (1964).

fat. In heavy exercise, however, although weight in terms of fat is lost, weight in terms of muscle growth may increase. Individuals who are relatively high in fat will tend to lose weight as a result of exercise. Individuals who are low in both fat and musculature may increase slightly in weight.

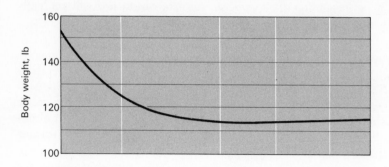

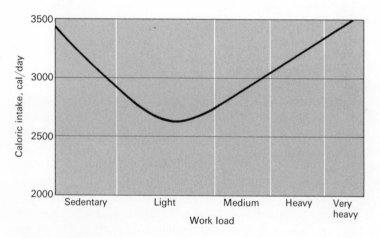

Fig. 2–9. Body weight and caloric intake for male employees at various work levels (data from an Oriental population). (a) In the group surveyed, the workers with the most sedentary jobs ate more than workers in jobs requiring light physical exertion. For workers with medium to heavy work loads, however, caloric intake rose in proportion to work load. (b) The sedentary workers also tended to weigh the most, with proportionally lower weight evident in workers with light and medium work loads. By contrast, the average weight of workers doing various degrees of heavy work was low despite their higher caloric intake. (Adapted by permission of the publisher from J. Mayer, P. Roy, and K. P. Mitra, "Relation between caloric intake, body weight, and physical work; studies in industrial male population in West Bengal." *American Journal of Clinical Nutrition* **4,** 169 (1956).

Many students are concerned about losing weight in certain areas of the body. This is not easily accomplished. The findings from scientific research on the effects of localized exercise as compared with general exercise* indicate that the energy supply demanded by *any* exercise is obtained from fatty deposits *throughout* the body. Although some areas of the body may change noticeably at the beginning of an exercise regimen, weight loss will gradually distribute itself equally throughout the body.

RESPIRATORY-CIRCULATORY FUNCTIONS

In the preceding section, respiration was defined and viewed in relation to metabolic processes in the body. In this section, respiration will be viewed in relation to the circulatory system and to some of the factors that control circulation as the body adapts to the physiological stress imposed by vigorous physical activity.

The need for maintenance of a constant, adequate supply of oxygen for the body tissues has been indicated previously. You can live for many days without food, but for only a few minutes if deprived of oxygen. Respiration and circulation work together to provide a constant supply of oxygen to the body tissues.

The circulatory system is composed of four basic anatomical structures: (a) the *heart*, (b) *arteries*, which carry blood away from the heart, (c) *veins*, which carry blood toward the heart, and (d) *capillaries*, the tiny, thin-walled blood vessels that are interposed between the arteries and veins, and in which occurs the exchange of materials between blood and body tissues or (in the lung) between blood and alveolar air (air in the terminal air sacs of the lungs).

The function of the heart is to keep blood flowing throughout the circulatory system. The system is so organized that it has two major component systems: *pulmonary* and *systemic* (see Fig. 2–10).

The pulmonary system serves to carry nonoxygenated blood from the right side of the heart to the lungs. The exchange of carbon dioxide and oxygen takes place between the cell walls of the capillaries and the air in the alveoli of the lungs. The veins from the lungs carry oxygenated blood from the lungs back to the left side of the heart.

The systemic system serves all the other tissues of the body. The regulation of blood flow through the systemic system depends on the need for oxygen and other nutrients in the body tissues. When the body is at rest, the skeletal muscles apparently account for not more than about 20% of the blood's total oxygen consumption. Substantial amounts of oxygen go to the brain, the heart, the skin, the kidneys, and other organs. During vigorous

---

* See Marie L. Carnes *et al.*, "Segmental volume reduction: localized versus generalized exercise." *Human Biology* **32**, 370–376 (1960).

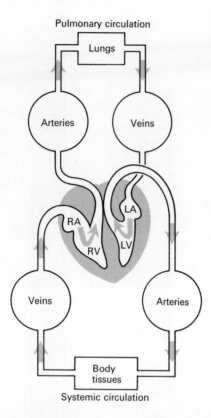

Pulmonary circulation

Systemic circulation

Fig. 2–10. Schematic representation of the cardiovascular system.

activity, however, such as running, skiing, and swimming, the active muscles need about 50 times their resting requirement. The other organs of the body do not require anywhere near as great an increase of oxygen during maximal exertion. Therefore, the oxygen requirements of skeletal muscles during vigorous activity can be met by appropriate alterations in the pattern of blood flow. Most of the arterial blood can be diverted from the other organs to the active muscles, where the need for oxygen is most acute.

Figure 2–11 shows that such changes in the pattern of blood flow do take place during vigorous activity. The figure also reveals that the rate of flow is proportional to the intensity of the physical activity. This circulatory adaptation is a function of both the *stroke volume* (the amount of blood ejected by the heart per beat) and the frequency or *rate* of each beat. Multiplication of the heart rate by the stroke volume yields the *cardiac output*, expressed here in milliliters of blood per minute. As may be seen in Fig. 2–11, the cardiac output when the body is at rest is 5800 ml/min. When physical activity increases to the level of maximal exertion, the cardiac output increases to 25,000 ml/min. In such conditions, the heart rate may only double, while the stroke volume increases to more than 200 times its resting

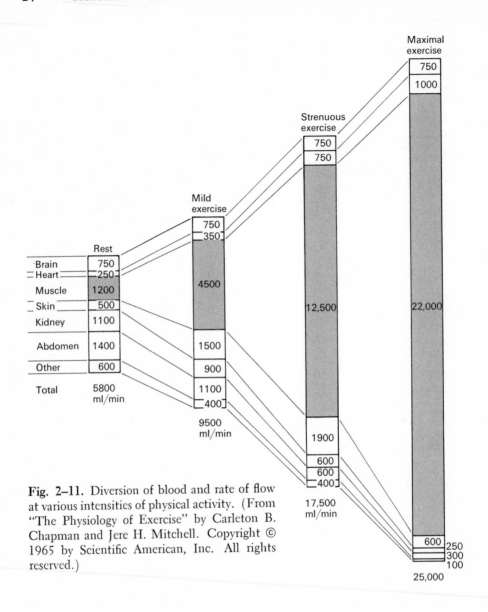

Fig. 2–11. Diversion of blood and rate of flow at various intensities of physical activity. (From "The Physiology of Exercise" by Carleton B. Chapman and Jere H. Mitchell. Copyright © 1965 by Scientific American, Inc. All rights reserved.)

value. This particular circulatory adaptation will be discussed again in Chapter 8, in relation to conditioning and the development of cardiovascular-respiratory endurance.

The contraction of skeletal muscles exerts a mechanical effect on blood flow. The contracting muscle fibers apparently exert pressure on the blood vessels in the muscle tissue. This has the effect of increasing blood flow in the veins while impeding the inflow from the arteries. When relaxation occurs, blood surges from the arteries into the emptied capillary beds in the muscles, and inflow is accelerated while outflow is temporarily retarded. Thus the muscles themselves act as a pump. (This effect has been referred to as the "milking action" of skeletal muscles.) For example, the slight sway of the body during standing posture (and associated contraction and relaxation of certain muscles of the lower legs) has been shown to be an important physiological adaptation of the body that assists in pumping blood from the extremities back to the heart.

An individual who becomes physically exhausted may find himself forced to give up some form of vigorous physical activity because of a feeling of "being out of breath." Even under such conditions, there is apparently an adequate supply of oxygen in the lungs. The inability to continue the activity lies in the inadequacy of some aspect of oxygen transport in the circulatory system. One such condition appears to be related to the amount of oxygen that can be absorbed by the blood as it moves through the lungs. During activity, blood moves faster through the lungs than while the body is at rest. Apparently, in some individuals the speed increases so much that the blood cannot pick up its normal quota of oxygen.* In such cases, there are definite limitations imposed on the level of physical activity in which the individual may engage.

The complexity of the mechanisms involved in the control of respiration and circulation goes far beyond what we have attempted to indicate in this text. For a complete explanation of the processes involved, you should refer to a general text on physiological functions in the human body. Several such references are given at the end of this chapter.

SUMMARY

1. The performance of physical activities requires the integrated functioning of all the body tissues. The bones of the body articulate at joints and are attached to other body parts by connective as well as muscle tissue. Movement is effected by muscular contraction as a result of stimulation by motor nerve fibers. The type of motion that results is determined not only by the particular muscles that are stimulated and the strength of the stimulus, but also by the structure of the joint where articulation occurs.

2. Because of the location of the muscle's attachment on the bone in relation to the axis of rotation and the point of resistance, in many movement activities a mechanical advantage is gained by increasing the length of the acting lever. Greater strength may become necessary, however, as the muscle is required to overcome a greater resistance.

---

* See Peter V. Karpovich, *Physiology of Muscular Activity*. Philadelphia: W. B. Saunders Company, 1966.

3. The energy for muscular contraction is derived from the oxidation of foodstuffs. Although food can be stored in the body for later use, there is no such reserve for oxygen. The circulatory system of the individual therefore plays an important part in determining the ability of the individual to engage in vigorous physical activity. During vigorous activity, the oxygen requirement of the body increases. To provide for an adequate supply of oxygen to the skeletal muscles where the oxygen need is most acute, there is a change in the pattern as well as in the rate of flow.

4. The physiological fitness of the individual plays an important part in determining the efficiency with which the body tissues can adapt to the stress imposed by vigorous physical activity.

SUGGESTED READING

CHAPMAN, CARLETON B., AND JERE H. MITCHELL, "The physiology of exercise." *Scientific American* 212, 88–96 (1965)

GUYTON, ARTHUR C., *Function of the Human Body*. Philadelphia: W. B. Saunders Company, 1965

HUXLEY, H. E., "The mechanism of muscular contraction." *Scientific American* 213, 18–27 (1965)

KARPOVICH, PETER V., *Physiology of Muscular Activity*. Philadelphia: W. B. Saunders Company, 1966

MAYER, JEAN, "Exercise and weight control," in *Science and Medicine of Exercise and Sports*, edited by Warren R. Johnson. New York: Harper & Row, 1960

STACY, RALPH W., AND JOHN A. SANTOLUCITO, *Modern College Physiology*. St. Louis: The C. V. Mosby Company, 1966

chapter 3
PHYSICAL LAWS AND
HUMAN STRUCTURE

Everything that moves and everything that is at rest obeys certain physical laws—and you are no exception! In physics, investigators in the area of mechanics have learned much about the nature of motion and the conditions of equilibrium, and have established certain principles that describe these states. Since your body is subject to the same laws as those which govern the motions of the universe, the principles of mechanics are applicable to your activities. Although you cannot change these laws, by understanding them you can, to a certain extent, increase your efficiency in many movement activities.

DESCRIPTION OF MOTION

Motion may be defined as a continuous change of position. An accurate description of a moving body, then, requires some method of identifying *position*, as well as a method of determining the duration of *time between successive positions*. From the basic information related to position and time, one can devise ways of measuring the speed, velocity, and acceleration of the moving body.

Since movement of your body can take place only at a joint, your body position and change of position are generally described in relation to joint actions and to the resulting relative displacement of your body segments. (A summary of the principal joint actions has already been given, in Chapter 2.) But many of the movements that you perform are so rapid and complex that unless you have at your disposal such aids as slow-motion film records, neither you nor an observer of your performance can analyze the many details of position or changes of position occurring throughout the entire performance of an action. Instead, you must usually make evaluations by observing the outcome of body movement—e.g., the speed, distance, flight, or rebound

27

of a ball; the position of the body as it enters the water from a dive; or the position of the body as it recovers from a stunt on the trampoline. From observation of the outcome and a knowledge of principles of mechanics it is possible to determine logical changes that should occur during the execution phase of the action in order to improve your performance of the skill.

FORCE

A force is necessary to overcome an object's *inertia* (the object's resistance to change of state). This applies either to an object already in motion or to an object in a state of rest, for the latter is simply a special case of motion —namely, zero motion. Thus, to restate the principle: a force is required to change either the speed or direction in which an object is moving.

In the seventeenth century, such men as Descartes, Leibnitz, and Newton sought to refine the familiar idea of force, which we today commonly call push or pull. The principles that were formalized at that time are all related in some way to the mass of the object acting or being acted on, the range or distance through which the movement occurs, and the direction of the application of the force.

The forces that govern your movements may originate within your body (from muscular contractions) or outside your body. An outside force that acts on your body may act to facilitate the movement or may require your body to counteract it.

The most persistent of the outside forces that are constantly acting on us, and on objects projected by our bodies, is the force of gravity. All objects within the earth's gravitational field are constantly subjected to this force, which is exerted in a vertical direction downward toward the center of the earth. The greater the mass of the object, the stronger the force of that pull. The magnitude of the force of gravitational attraction that the earth exerts on an object is called the *weight* of the object.

Gravity acts on all points of any object. It is the distribution of these points in space that determines the location of the *center of gravity* of the object—that is, the point of concentration of mass, or more simply, the point in relation to which all parts of the object are in balance. In the case of a symmetrical body with uniform density, such as a ball or block, the geometrical center is also the center of gravity. Since the human body is irregularly shaped and has many movable parts, its center of gravity cannot be so easily defined; moreover, it is subject to change with every change in position of the body or a body part. When you are in the normal standing position with your arms hanging at your sides, your center of gravity (if you are an adult female) is located at a distance approximately 55% of your total standing height from the floor. (This distance will vary somewhat, depending on your body build.) In general, then, the center of gravity in the human body in standing position can be thought of as being in the region of the hips.

Now, what happens when an object or the body is acted on by two forces (such as muscular effort working with or against the force of gravity)? The movement then will be in the direction of the *resultant* of the two force. The greatest efficiency in movement is, of course, achieved when all forces are in the direction of the intended motion.

If linear motion is desired (and an object or the body is free to move), the force should be applied through the center of gravity of the object or body. Linear motion will *not* result if an object is fixed at some point, or if force is applied off-center of the object. Instead, rotary motion will result. The farther from the center of gravity the force is applied, the less force will be necessary to rotate the object.

THE LAWS OF MOTION

Newton formulated three laws of motion. Newton's second law states that the rate of change of momentum is proportional to the unbalanced force and is in the direction of that force. (Momentum is the product of mass and velocity). For example, given an object of a certain mass, the greater the force applied to it, the greater will be the velocity (and the momentum) of the object in the direction of the applied force. Thus, to increase either velocity or momentum, force must be increased proportionately.

Newton's first law states that an object that is at rest or in motion will remain at rest or in motion at the same speed, in a straight line, unless acted on by a force. This law, when viewed against the background of the second law, is simply a special case of the second.* That is, if the force is zero, the acceleration is also necessarily zero, and the speed is therefore constant. An alteration of motion, whether in speed or in direction, requires the application of a force; in the absence of any force, neither kind of alteration will occur.

These first two laws of Newton have implications for all movements of the human body. A force must be applied whenever it is necessary to overcome the body's inertia. This is true whether the body is at rest or already in motion. It is common to experience greater difficulty in starting an object in motion, or to alter its direction once it is already in motion, than it is to maintain a constant magnitude and direction of motion. The circular path used during the backswing in tennis strokes provides the player with an efficient means of overcoming the inertia of the racket as the

---

* See Francis Weston Sears and Mark W. Zemansky, *College Physics*. Reading, Mass.: Addison-Wesley Publishing Company, Inc., 1960.

direction of the motion is changed. The greater the mass of an object, the greater must be the force to overcome the inertia. Greater strength may be required to swing a heavier racket or club, or to roll a heavier bowling ball. With a constant force, however, the less the mass of the object, the greater will be its velocity. There comes a point, however, when because of the smallness of the mass of the object or because of the object's design, other forces must be taken into consideration. This is particularly evident in the flight characteristics of a badminton bird, where air resistance is a significant factor.

Newton's third law states that to every action there is always opposed an equal reaction. The decisive factor on the impact of two objects is momentum. This has already been defined as mass times velocity. Momentum possesses not only magnitude but also direction, the latter being determined by the direction of the velocity involved. For example, when you are running, you apply successive backward pushes with your feet against the ground; the reaction to these movements is what produces your forward motion. Because of the earth's tremendous mass and velocity, you have no effect on the direction or velocity of the earth—which is extremely fortunate for all concerned!

Because of Newton's third law, when it becomes necessary for your body to absorb force there should be a gradual reduction of momentum (accomplished by reduction of force) over a long time and over a long distance. Should you trip and fall, for example, there is less likelihood that you will be injured if you accomplish a gradual reduction of momentum over as large an area of your body surface as is practical.

EQUILIBRIUM

An object is in a state of equilibrium or rest when the resultant of all forces acting on it is zero—that is, when a force from any given direction is balanced by an equal force from the opposite direction. An imbalance of forces will cause either a linear or rotary motion, depending on the point at which the force is applied.

The equilibrium of a body is said to be *stable* if, on being slightly displaced, the body tends to return to its original position; the equilibrium is *unstable* if the body tends, instead, to move farther from that position. Equilibrium depends primarily on the location of the center of gravity in relation to the supporting base and the direction of the forces involved. Stability and instability are involved in all forms of human activity; a knowledge of the mechanical principles related to equilibrium can be used to produce the state of equilibrium required. However, it is unwise to adopt any single principle without considering it in the full context of the situation in which the body is involved.

Broad base, stable equilibrium
easily maintained

Narrow base, stable equilibrium
less easily maintained

Fig. 3–1. Geometric forms illustrating principles of equilibrium in relation to center of gravity, line of gravity, and base of support.

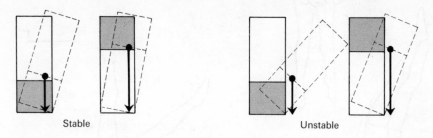

Stable   Unstable

Fig. 3–2. Geometric forms illustrating principles of equilibrium in relation to concentration of mass, line of gravity, and support.

The following basic principles of equilibrium are illustrated in Figs. 3–1 and 3–2 in relation to simple geometric forms:

1. An object is stable when its center of gravity is directly over its supporting base. The nearer to the center of that base the line of gravity falls, the less likely it is that the object will become unstable.

2. An object with a large base of support tends to remain stable more easily than one with a small base of support.

3. If, when the object is displaced, the line of gravity of the object remains *within* the supporting base, then the equilibrium is stable and the object will return to its original neutral position.

4. If, when the object is displaced, the line of gravity of the object falls *outside* the base of support, then the equilibrium is unstable and the object will seek a new base until stable equilibrium is achieved.

5. Depending on the distribution of mass of an object, the lower in space the concentration of mass, the farther the object must be tipped before it loses stability.

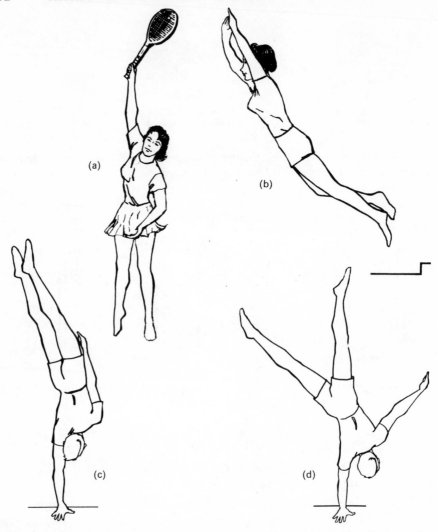

Fig. 3–3. Examples of the body in relatively unstable positions. (a) High center of gravity. (b) Center of gravity falls outside of the base of support. (c) Body is supported over a small base of support. (d) Greater distribution of mass over a small base of support.

The principles of equilibrium in relation to the human body engaged in various sports activities are illustrated in Figs. 3–3 and 3–4. Your body, un-like the geometric forms just discussed, is capable of generating its own force, and consideration must be given to determine the "best" position to control this force as well as to control external opposing forces. For greater stability, your supporting base should be enlarged in the direction of the moving or opposing force. The lunge step and slide on the last step in bowling, the forward stride in throwing, and the lunge in fencing are examples of the

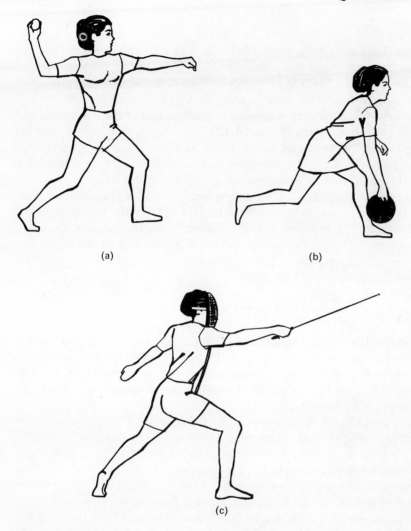

Fig. 3–4. Examples of the body in relatively stable positions. The center of gravity is lowered over a wide base of support with a stride in the direction of the movement.

adjustments used to overcome body momentum acquired in the process of applying force to the body itself. You should assume a stride stance in the direction of the opposing force when you wish to move a heavy object, to combat a gale wind, or to adjust to changes in motion which occur when you stand in a moving vehicle such as a train or bus.

If a part of the body such as a leg or an arm moves away from the line of gravity in one direction, the center of gravity shifts in that direction. Or if external weights are lifted by or added to the body, the weight becomes a part of the total body weight and the location of the center of gravity is displaced in the direction of the added weight. When you are carrying a heavy object, the closer to the line of gravity you hold the weight, the less effort you will expend to hold it. In an activity such as bowling, swinging the ball as close to the line of gravity as possible in the direction of the movement will keep the body from being displaced laterally. Body adjustments such as bending at the hip joint and at the knees have the effect of lowering the center of gravity in the body. Providing that the supporting base remains the same or increases, such adjustments aid in stabilizing the body.

In general, maintaining a large supporting base and a low center of gravity and keeping the line of gravity close to the center of the base provide for greatest stability. If, however, a stable position is not desired, just the opposite conditions will be required: the center of gravity should be raised, the base narrowed, and the line of gravity moved in the direction of the edge of the supporting base.

Buoyancy

The utility of the concept of equilibrium is not limited to solid bases but is applicable in relation to fluids as well. In fact, the concept was applied to liquids about 2000 years before it appeared in the mechanics of solids. The first formulation of the principle of equilibrium in liquids was made by Archimedes (287–212 B.C.).

What is known as Archimedes' principle states that "a body immersed in a fluid is buoyed up with a force equal to the weight of the fluid displaced." When a body is immersed either wholly or partly in a fluid, obviously a certain amount of fluid is displaced. The effect of the pressure that the fluid exerts on the body is an upward force that tends to partially offset the downward pull of gravity. It can be shown that this force, called a *buoyant* force, is equal in magnitude to the weight of the fluid displaced. Therefore, if the weight of a body is less than the weight of the volume of fluid that it would displace when submerged, then the body will float in the fluid; conversely, if it is heavier than the same volume of the fluid, it will sink.

Since Archimedes' principle considers only the conditions under which bodies will float—the so-called translational equilibrium of floating bodies—the conditions must be specified under which bodies will float and yet not rotate.

An object has a center of buoyancy in the same sense that it has a center of gravity. The center of buoyancy is the center of gravity of the displaced volume of water. It is the point around which the upward buoying force of the water is equally distributed. Since the center of gravity is the point around which the downward pull of gravity is equally distributed, the two forces are in exact opposition. If the two centers should happen to coincide, the swimmer will float in a horizontal position (if the swimmer is buoyant enough to float at all). However, in most individuals the center of buoyancy is nearer the head than the center of gravity is, and therefore the feet usually sink. This sinking represents a rotation of the body around the center of buoyancy. Rotation will continue until the center of gravity is directly under the center of buoyancy. The farther apart these two points are, the greater must be the rotation to produce the effect of equilibrium. Adjustments in floating (see Chapter 10) are merely attempts to bring these two points into alignment.

Mechanisms for Maintaining Equilibrium

There are several ways in which your central nervous system is informed of the orientation of your body in space and thus can make you aware of your state of equilibrium. Vision, the balance mechanisms of the inner ear, the proprioceptive sense organs, and the end organs which mediate deep pressure are important sense organs for maintaining balance. In addition to gaining a conceptual understanding of the principles of equilibrium, it is important that you become aware of the feeling of your body in various positions and to attend to the sensations provided by your various sense modalities. This topic will be further considered in Chapter 5.

SUMMARY

1. A force is required to overcome the inertia of an object.
2. Forces which govern motion of the human body may originate within the body (from muscular contraction) or from outside the body.
3. The most persistent of the outside forces that are constantly acting on us, and on all objects projected by our bodies, is the force of gravity.
4. The greatest efficiency in movement is achieved when all forces are in the direction of the intended motion.
5. Newton's laws describe characteristics of objects in motion. These laws are also applicable to motion of the human body.
6. An object acts (or is acted upon) as if its entire mass were located at the center of gravity. Since the human body is irregularly shaped and has many movable parts, the position of the center of gravity changes with every change in position of the body or of a body segment.
7. The state of equilibrium of the human body depends on the height of the center of gravity in the body, the location of the line of gravity in relation to the base of support, and the size of the supporting base.
8. The adjustments of the position of the body, when immersed in water, will depend both on the location of the center of gravity and the center of

buoyancy. Adjustments in floating are a result of rotation of the center of gravity about the center of buoyancy.

9. Various sense organs of the body play an important role in the maintenance of stable equilibrium.

SUGGESTED READING

BROER, MARION R., *Efficiency of Human Movement*. Philadelphia: W. B. Saunders Company, 1966

DYSON, GEOFFREY H. G., *The Mechanics of Athletics*. London: University of London Press, 1964

NAPIER, JOHN, "The antiquity of human walking." *Scientific American* **216**, 56–66 (1967)

WILLIAMS, MARIAN, AND HERBERT R. LISSNER, *Biomechanics of Human Motion*. Philadelphia: W. B. Saunders Company, 1962

chapter 4
MOVEMENT AND CULTURE

We have identified many partial answers to our initial question concerning why human beings move as they do. Some "answers" have involved anatomical-structural phenomena, and some have been concerned with the physical environment. There is yet another potent shaping force in the movement experiences of human beings—the socio-cultural context of movement behavior. The term "socio-cultural context" here refers to the sum total of the influences of all environmental objects in the perceptual field of the individual.

The concept of the complete interrelatedness of the individual and his society is well supported. Some writers prefer to use the hyphenated term "individual-in-his-environment" (excluding the use of either *individual* or *environment* as separate entities), in order to indicate the dynamic, inseparable, interactive nature of these phenomena. It is possible to view human movement experiences as similarly interrelated with the socio-cultural context.

In this chapter we shall consider the interrelation of movement and culture from two vantage points. The first views movement as a language of culture. The second views the culture itself as a "thesaurus" for movement experiences.

MOVEMENT: THE FIRST LANGUAGE OF CULTURE

It may seem unusual to consider a nonverbal "language," but there is much information to substantiate a view of human movement activities as *first communications* in any culture.

But before we delve further into movement as language it is important to identify the meaning of the term culture within the context of our discussion. Some things seem to exist rather concretely and discretely in the so-called real world; for example, it is relatively easy to point out apples, pencils, or trees. Culture does not exist in quite the same concrete form, however, and so a truly definitive statement would be potentially infinite. For our purposes let us assume that what *we* mean by the term culture is the *totality of learned behavior* of a people existing together in time and space. The conceptualization of the phrase "totality of learned behaviors" is staggering when one considers that this includes, for example, religious patterns, educational patterns, work patterns, and movement patterns. Even if we should limit the learned behaviors to *movement behavior* we encompass a universe of responses.

We believe, for instance, that the impulse to walk is built into the human system; unless his environment is excessively depriving, the child will locomote on two feet with the hands free. But the *manner* of walking—the speed, length of gait, and degree of energy expended—is tremendously influenced by the culture that surrounds the child and the models presented for him to imitate.

Movement as Communication Within Cultures

Movement is a preverbal language. Much is communicated to children, much is learned by children before they master the abstract symbolism of speech. Anthropologists give many classic examples to show that early movement experiences communicate a great deal to the child about the society in which he finds himself. Certain peoples produce cooperating, responsive individuals whose greatest joys lie in their relationships with their children. Babies are treated as soft, vulnerable, precious objects, to be protected and cherished. Little or nothing may be demanded of them. By the age of three or four, a hypothetical child in such a culture might be well oriented to a quiet, passive, yet generous manner of response. Other societies pit human beings against each other, man, woman, and child alike. Aggression and challenge might form a major portion of a child's activities in such a society. Thus movement activities are a means of communicating cultural orientation long before the child understands the abstract symbolism of speech.

Movement as a Source of Information About a Culture

There is, perhaps, another sense in which movement is a first language of culture. Anthropological research is often concerned with (a) the identification of certain primary patterns within the culture, and (b) the comparison of the form of the pattern across cultures. Some of the primary areas mentioned above, and which are directly and heavily involved with human movement, might be work patterns, play, and protection or defense.* By studying the movement patterns inherent in a culture's habits in these areas, we can describe the culture to some degree, no matter when it appeared in human history, no matter in what section of the world it flourished. Habitual movement patterns become, then, a language *describing* any given culture.

Let us consider for a moment the primitive man of western Europe. From what we know of him, his movement experiences centered around hunting (his subsistence), dance rituals (defense against evil spirits, or perhaps play), and fighting. His primary concern was coping with the hostile environment. We see bison through the eyes of Man the Hunter in the cave paintings of France. The movement of the animal (and matching that movement) was so important that the primitive artist tried to illustrate the motion by putting many legs on the bison, almost in the manner of present-day cartooning techniques.

Let us move on from primitive man and consider the records we have from classical Greece. Man's image of himself had been greatly extended. The Greek citizen saw man, in the ideal, as a creature exemplifying perfect symmetry of mind, body, and soul. Great gymnasia were erected for the disciplining of all three. The statue *The Discus Thrower* illustrates the perfection of the Greek ideal. Unfortunately, there seem to be no female counterparts to *The Discus Thrower*. The Athenian woman was virtually a slave, with her movement experiences limited to household tasks. The Spartan woman was slightly more free, her physical skills more emphasized, but this was because she was to be the mother of warriors (an orientation also seen in Nazi Germany prior to World War II). Nevertheless, for the Greek male citizen, man and his movements were unified as they had never been before and as they would not be again for many centuries.

The Judeo-Christian taboos about the impurity and evilness of the body greatly reduced man's opportunities (even as a child) to move and to play, especially during the period roughly extending from 1000 to 1700 A.D. This basic orientation against any movement activity with connotations of "play" was very noticeable in our own early American literature and history, so heavily influenced by Judeo-Christian tradition. To find an orientation where recreation and movement activities were beginning to be valued we must move to the turn of the twentieth century. The technological breakthroughs of the industrial revolution were freeing men, women, and children from the burdens of dawn-to-dusk subsistence movements and leaving them the time and social freedom to truly enjoy themselves.

This brief review indicates in a cursory manner the way in which specific cultures may be described in terms of their movement activities. There is yet

---

* See Edward T. Hall, *The Silent Language.* Greenwich, Conn.: Fawcett Publications, 1959.

another reason for suggesting that movement is a first language of culture. The activities of the young, in any culture, may be seen as life situations in miniature, where children or young adults can "practice responses" and determine which ways of responding are most efficient and satisfying. The "game" is designed to be symbolic of life and the individuals who play learn much about themselves and others through the experience. Again we see individuals learning about their social surroundings by participation in movement-centered activities.

Nature of the Language of Movement

We have identified certain benefits for the individual when the movement language is well learned and extensive, and also the ways in which societies, through time, have utilized movement learning for indoctrination of the young. Let us consider now the most basic concern, the delineation of the exact nature of this silent language. Since movement behaviors exist as a silent mode of communications across cultures, we could, perhaps, understand our fellow human beings more fully if we would attend carefully, not only to the meaning of their words, but also to the meaning of their movements. What, then, are the possible modes of human communication or expression centering in movement?

In attempts to know another individual and his situation there are many personality factors that must be considered, but usually a beginning communication is established at first glance through *facial expression* and *body pose* or *postures*. Another mode of expression is *gesture*—the wave "hello-goodby," the outstretched hand. These may relate volumes.

The manner in which a person *utilizes space* and *time* is also a movement-oriented method of communication. Whether the individual moves quickly, slowly, expansively, inhibitedly, all give clues to the status of the individual. E. T. Hall, in his book *The Silent Language*, provides penetrating insight to space-time-movement communication on the total societal level, while some of Rudolf Laban's work approaches the same question from an individualistic framework.

The last mode of communication through movement is that of the *art form*—that of dance: ballet, modern or contemporary, and folk dance when it is structured as formal art. We shall refer to this subject at greater length in Chapters 6 and 12.

CULTURE: A THESAURUS FOR MOVEMENT EXPERIENCES

An English thesaurus is, as you know, filled with possibilities of words that we may select to use in a given situation. It enables us to find the *proper* word to fill our need.

Similarly, one's culture, to a great extent, draws expectations for one that affect the movement experiences and habits seeming "proper" or perhaps even "necessary." In this respect, one's culture becomes a thesaurus, filled with possibilities of movement patterns that may be selected in a given situation. From the movement patterns perceived as "culturally acceptable," the individual selects the ones that fill his needs. As he grows, matures, accepts the cultural expectations, and performs in accordance with them, he *becomes* a possible cultural model for his own children.

How do we come to know what expectancies are held for us in the area of movement behavior? How is the movement thesaurus made known? The answer seems so incredibly simple as to be almost unworthy of mention; we *learn* what constitutes acceptable movement behaviors, we are *taught* painstakingly. But the apparent simplicity is deceptive. We learn about acceptable movement behavior as a subset of a larger concern: what constitutes a total pattern of acceptable behavior for a woman, for a man? What constitutes femininity, masculinity? Sometimes, in the process of learning a sex role, we get the idea that there is "a model" for each sex, known and agreed upon by all. However, there seems to be no consensus of this type.

Let us, in our thinking, differentiate "maleness-femaleness" from "masculinity-femininity." We may define maleness-femaleness as a status established at conception and independent of such factors as nationality, social class, religion, or degree of education. Masculinity-femininity seems, on the other hand, essentially learned, not set rigidly by our biology. The anthropological studies of Mead and others indicate that dramatic shifts in what is considered "masculine" or "feminine" may occur from culture to culture.

This brings us again to a question, how does "masculinization" or "femininization" in movement behaviors occur in our society?

Selective Rewards and Punishments

One way this learning occurs is through the selective rewards and punishments of parents, relatives, and friends. All the individuals with whom the child interacts hold beliefs or expectancies for the child, and he is treated very differently depending on whether he chooses what seems the correct or incorrect response. For example, some mothers are so fearful for their children, so over-protecting, that throughout the child's attempts to explore his world he is continually cautioned or even punished for his daring. Such a child may tend to grow up feeling that the environment is rather threatening or even hostile, and as a result he may assiduously avoid the exploration of his world through movement. If the child is a girl, she may be reinforced in these feelings by the cultural definitions of acceptable behaviors for females.

What does it mean to "throw like a girl"? There may be other subtle ways in which rewards and punishments that are offered in our culture work against a girl's capacity for moving. A trip to the department store toy shop will reveal the world's *largest* stock of "sit down," "play house-wife" appliances. How often do girls past the age of 9 receive as gifts such movement-demanding objects as balls, kites, pogo sticks, or skate boards?

It may be, however, that the most powerful influence that is brought to bear in the movement role-learning of girls in our culture is the assigning of all skill and efficiency in movement to boys. As surely as we find a girl who experiences real joy in her throwing, catching, turning, jumping, we will find a voice saying to her (in words and deeds), "My, you throw like a boy," or "You swing on that limb just like a little boy." At worst, the little girl may come to feel that there is something wrong in her which causes her to derive so much pleasure from her vigorous activity. She may withdraw from her achievement in games with a degree of bitterness in her heart for the sex role that has cost her a very human joy. Or, she may somewhat defensively continue her movement activities, feeling keenly a discrepancy between herself and other girls. At its best, the taboo on skilled movement for women is a gentle, patronizing voice saying, "Be a cute little tomboy now, for the time will soon come when you will put these things aside and be about the really important task of being a woman." Perhaps the only plight worse than that of the girl who "throws like a boy" is that of the poor young fellow whose misfortune it is to "throw like a girl."

Male lion, rabbit, grasshopper—which can jump the highest? The previous discussion may illustrate a way of thinking described by Margaret Mead* as being almost habitual in our culture, that is, to see masculinity-femininity as a single continuum, with the most masculine and most feminine at opposite poles. All individuals with whom interaction occurs are then ranked, and reranked periodically, in relation to certain dimensions of this continuum. Let us assume, for example, that the human potential for experiencing pleasure and self-identification through highly vigorous activity may be perceived in our culture as a dimension of masculinity-femininity. The "most masculine" man would experience the greatest pleasure in vigorous activity. The woman who derived great joy from highly vigorous activity would therefore be reflecting a masculine attribute. The "most feminine" woman would not wish to pursue such activities.

Dr. Mead questions this single-continuum concept. She points out that there are male rabbits, turtles, lions, and kangaroos, and asks whether it is possible to group them as males and then rank them all on the basis of their jumping ability. If we must compare the attributes of men and women, could we not visualize *types* of men and women and compare them in this

---

* See Margaret Mead, *Male and Female*. New York: New American Library, 1964.

fashion? Is it not possible, on the basis of interest, skills, and/or body configuration, to postulate an aesthetic type of man *or* woman, or an athletic type? The "athletic" woman would be quite well differentiated from the "athletic" man. She would be tremendously skilled and yet never pose a threat to his masculinity. Neither would she threaten the masculinity sphere of the aesthetic man. Is the male lion red-faced about the high-jumping kangaroo? Obviously there are no men and women who could be categorized exactly in this manner, but this model does seem to take into account more human differences than a simple uni-model comparison of *all* men with *all* women.

Imitation of Models

We have been dealing with the way in which people learn the movement role they consider to be proper in relation to one cultural stereotype that equates skill in movement with masculinity.

If this were the only influence to be considered the task would be relatively easy. There are conflicting influences present in our complex culture, however, and it is possible to study some of these influences in relation to another method of role-learning, the imitation of models.

The child and the young adult learn what is acceptable movement behavior by watching and copying the guides whom they perceive about them. The first and foremost guides and models are the parents of the child, and the inconsistencies of parents' demands in our culture have been catalogued by many sociologists. We have already suggested a possible cultural stereotype that would have all men skillful and vigorous and all women much less so. In conflict with this orientation is the heavy American emphasis on success and achievement. Little distinction is made in what children wear and little distinction (in younger children) is made in what games they play at school. Boys and girls alike are encouraged to compete, to succeed, to achieve. Parents may be rather anxious about making sure their children have every chance to do all three. As Mead has indicated, American parents are primarily concerned with their children's status, not as members of one sex or the other, but as potential high achievers. This seems to be the school orientation probably up through the 7th or 8th grade. From the period of puberty on, however, being "manly" (the cultural thesaurus tells us this means superior) becomes of primary importance to the boy and being "feminine" (winning too many games would not be appropriate here) is equally important for the girl. Mead suggests that girls usually respond by rejecting the dilemma, avoiding the game "where winning means losing." One must wonder if such an either-or choice is necessary.

POSSIBLE EFFECTS OF CULTURAL DETERMINANTS

In the previous discussion some of the methods by which men and women take on culturally expected movement activity habits have been considered. Once these habits are assumed, what are their effects upon our people? What differences among individuals does research suggest may be caused, in part, by cultural determinants?

1. Clear delineation of expected role-behaviors seems not to be found in most of our culture. In certain of the more traditional Indian or Latin American cultures there would probably be little conflict about whether or not girls and women should play or compete vigorously or to what degree this should be allowed. It would simply not be considered generally acceptable. These types of movement possibilities would probably not appear in the "movement thesaurus." At the other extreme, it would appear that there would be little controversy about highly vigorous women in the U.S.S.R. It seems to be a national purpose to encourage women to extend themselves and excel wherever possible. In our country, both these extremes of opinion seem to exist, as well as many shades of opinion in between, with the result that each individual probably has a different "acceptable movement-model" for herself than any other of her peers.

2. In the early days of our country, recreation had to be rationalized in terms of work: barn-raising, house-warming, corn-husking. Our culture has developed technologically to a high degree and attitudes have changed enough since Puritan days so that recreation activities are not only acceptable, but highly esteemed. A *certain level* of skill seems to be a social value for a woman. In other cultures, in other times, the wife's role was to be in the service of her husband, to cook and sew and bear children. She was *not* "expected" to be his friend or companion. Companionship seems to be something of a marriage ideal in our present culture and there is a certain valuing of the woman who "thinks young" and has a zest for skiing, sailing, or swimming.

3. In one recent research effort, I.Q. test scores were collected for a group of children over a ten-year period. The data indicated that children who were described as passive, shy, and dependent exhibited a tendency toward dropping of I.Q. scores. Children described as competitive, self-assertive, and independent showed a tendency toward rising scores. There seem to be two points which bear possible investigation. First, movement exploration and problem-solving have been suggested as aids to the development of creativity and independence. It is possible that these activities should be more strongly encouraged for more children. Second, it should be recognized that self-

assertiveness, competitiveness, and independence are not commonly considered highly attractive feminine traits.*

Maccobey, in a section of Farber and Wilson's *The Potential of Women*, explicitly suggests that women's perceptual skills may be affected detrimentally by the dependence and submissiveness that is considered desired behavior.†

If we accept the idea that movement is a language of culture and culture is a thesaurus of movement, then should not *every* child be encouraged to develop and extend his own "vocabulary" to the very limits of his or her capacity, with the full support of the social structure, throughout the whole of life?

From this material, it is hoped that an important knowledge will have been gained. In the study of human personality, few but the naive would attempt to completely separate the individual from his environment. The two are believed to be mutually interacting phenomena. In a similar fashion, it seems impossible to separate movement behaviors and expectations from the cultural environment. The two are as intimately interrelated as moving and the human personality.

SUMMARY

1. Movement may be considered a preverbal mode of communication.
2. Certain aspects of given cultures may be described by movement behaviors and patterns.
3. General orientation toward movement activities varies with the general philosophies of the cultures concerned.
4. Communication through movement may take the form of facial expression, body posture, gesture, utilization of space and time, formal art forms.
5. The "culture" may affect the selection of movement patterns which are deemed acceptable by members of the culture.
6. Expectations of movement behavior may be learned by (a) a selective process of rewards and punishments and (b) imitation of models.
7. "Acceptable movement-models" probably vary greatly within the present-day United States.
8. Women's perceptual and movement skills may be detrimentally affected by certain of the "expected behavioral characteristics."

---

* See Seymour M. Farber and Roger H. L. Wilson, *The Potential of Women*. New York: McGraw-Hill Book Company, 1963.
† *Ibid.*

SUGGESTED READING

FARBER, SEYMOUR M., AND ROGER H. L. WILSON, *The Potential of Women.* New York: McGraw-Hill Book Company, 1963

HALL, EDWARD T., *The Silent Language.* Greenwich, Conn.: Fawcett Publications, 1959

KLUCKHOHN, CLYDE, *Mirror for Man.* New York: McGraw-Hill Book Company, 1940

MEAD, MARGARET, *Male and Female.* New York: New American Library, 1964

EXPERIMENTS IN MOVEMENT AS RELATED TO CULTURE

EXPRESSION OF IDEAS THROUGH MOVEMENT

Objectives

1. To experience the process of selecting the essence of an object, a person, or an event, and translating it into a movement-based expression.

2. To perceive the movement form of communication carried on by facial expression, posture or pose, and gesture.

Experiences

1. Identify the objects or processes that might be operative in an automated, autocratic future society (i.e., *1984* or *Brave New World*).

2. Identify how people might *feel* in this culture, especially in relation to the objects in #1 above.

3. Identify a movement or movement pattern descriptive or characteristic of one of the objects in #1 above.

4. Perform this movement or pattern while traveling through space.

5. Identify a movement or movement pattern expressing the human feelings described in #2 above.

6. Perform the two movement-ideas together.

MOVEMENT ACTIVITY AND CULTURAL VALUES

Objectives

1. To identify some values of our culture that are inherent in the rules and conduct of selected games and sports.

2. To explore and invent game forms which reflect selected hypothetical societal values.

Experiences

1. Differing values are reflected in the rules and conduct of tennis and basketball. Five points of difference are listed in Table 4–1, and the associated social values for three of these are commented on. Study the table and answer the questions on the following page.

TABLE 4–1 Comparison of Sports in Terms of Social Values

Basketball	Tennis	Associated social values
1. Invented in the United States and first played in highly competitive college sports atmosphere.	Imported from Europe and participation limited to the "genteel" for many years.	European concept of "gentleman" as opposed to the aggressive, win-the-best-way-you-can attitude perhaps necessary to the pioneer-frontiersman. Which one *do* we value? *Should* we value? Can we value both?
2. Generally, officiating is done by nonplayers and is rather firmly administered.	Officiating is at least shared by players and often they act as the only officials.	Concept of the honest, self-directing individual as opposed to need for strong central authority to make sure competition remains fair.
3. "Gamesmanship" or taking advantage of the rules is often overlooked or encouraged.	To maintain honor in play is highly valued.	Does "fair play" include trying to rattle opposing players or make them angry? Is it "their tough luck" if they have a lack of poise in this respect?
4. Coaches often take an active, if not dominant, part in strategy as the game progresses.	Coaches are not in evidence on the court as matches proceed.	
5. Fans are vigorous in shouting encouragement to their favorites and discouragement to the opposite team.	Fans are usually polite, rather impartial observers.	

a) What social values are reflected in the remaining two differences?

b) Can you add to the list of differences?

c) Devise a similar comparison chart for two other games.

2. With the equipment available to you, make up a game that reflects each of the hypothetical societies described in (a) through (d).

a) A culture located in a cold, mountainous environment where maintenance of morale and feelings of community are difficult.

b) A tense, fast-moving, scientifically oriented culture where individualism is highly valued.

c) A "have not" culture where aggressiveness is a necessity for self-preservation.

d) A culture where life is slow-paced, general participation in aesthetic experiences is encouraged, and self-expressiveness is a common trait.

chapter 5
MOVEMENT AND
PERCEPTION

If you were suddenly deprived of all sensation except that of vision how would you fare? Not too well, we would guess. Just think for a moment what this would really mean. You could no longer look at the world around you while you walked, for you would need to keep your vision focused on your feet and legs, to guide them where you wished to go. If you retained your vision and suddenly had the auditory sense returned to you, you would not be too much better off; you could even be provided with the senses of taste and smell in addition to sight and hearing, and though life might be a trifle more interesting, it would still be difficult. Why? Because you would still lack certain important sensory data that we all take for granted: the data supplied by your tactile and proprioceptive receptors. Thus you would be unable to distinguish hot from cold, strong pressures from weak ones, painful sensations from pleasant ones, and (unless you actually looked at them) you would be unable to tell whether your arms were over your head, behind your back, or at your sides. In short, you would be deprived of a great deal of information that you need in order to function effectively.

In the learning of movement activities, as in other areas of daily life, many people place greatest reliance on their vision, and thus fail to appreciate the importance of the role played by their other senses. In this chapter, therefore, we shall first examine sensory perception in general, and then discuss the role of vision as related to that of the other senses in movement activities. At the end of the chapter you will find a set of experiments designed to help you assess your ability to take cues from the various nonvisual sensory modes in the performance of movement tasks.

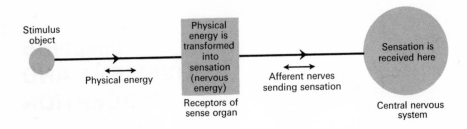

Fig. 5–1. Schematic representation of the pathway of a stimulus received by receptors and transformed into sensation.

SENSATION, PERCEPTION, AND MOTOR RESPONSES

We are constantly receiving numerous stimuli from objects and events in the external environment. In addition, we receive stimuli from our own internal environments. In fact, a constant supply of sensory data seems to be a necessity for maintenance of the integrity of the human organism. Experiments in sensory deprivation give some evidence that humans who have been cut off from as much sensory stimulation as possible over relatively short periods of time lose their awareness of body orientation, have hallucinations, and suffer certain personality aberrations.

Recall from Chapter 2 that data from all kinds of stimuli are collected by the receptors of the sense organs and travel in the form of nervous impulses over the afferent network of the nervous system to the brain. The brain performs the prodigious task of organizing all incoming information, together with appropriate stored data from past events, into a meaningful pattern—in light of which we make responses to the stimuli. If motor responses are required, for example, then impulses travel out from the brain, over the efferent network of the nervous system, to the muscle groups involved. Each response, in its own turn, acts as a stimulus that causes information to be transmitted back to the brain—again, over the afferent network. Evaluation of this "feedback" data results in a decision as to whether or not the response has been satisfactory. When the feedback from some response informs us that the mission in question has been satisfactorily accomplished, stimuli for that particular movement cease to be sent to the muscle groups concerned (see Figs. 5–1 and 5–2).

Thus, contrary to the popular notion, the brain does not function simply as a "central telephone exchange." That is, sensory stimuli are not tiny, discrete impulses that travel in some sort of linear order to the brain and there automatically set off another series of discrete, linear impulses of the same magnitude, to be sent out in linear order to various parts of the body.

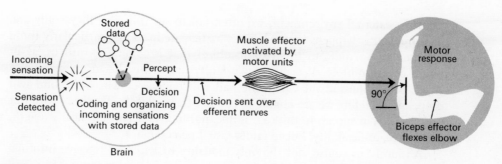

Fig. 5–2. Schematic representation of the process of perception and the resultant response.

Instead, incoming data arrive simultaneously from *several* sense modalities (vision, hearing, etc.) and seem to be organized by the brain into a *pattern* (something far more complex than a linear arrangement). On the basis of this pattern the brain determines the response, or the several simultaneous responses, that should be made.

For the purposes of our discussion, then, let us define *sensation* as the transformed energy of a stimulus that is received by the receptors and that travels over the afferent nerves of the central nervous system to the brain. And let us define *perception* as that organizing process which is an intermediate stage between sensation and response, the latter being caused by impulses sent out by the brain via the efferent nerves. In our discussion, however, we shall use the term "perception" more frequently to refer to the *product* of this organizing process that takes place in the brain—i.e., the *pattern* that is the basis for choice of responses. In this sense we may, for example, speak of "visual perception," "auditory perception," etc.

VISION IN RELATION TO OTHER SENSORY MODES

The responses we make to an object or situation depend on the way in which we perceive that object or situation. But our perceptions do not always correspond to events as they actually occur in the true or objective world. A classic illustration of this phenomenon is the variety of "factual" statements that can be gathered from various witnesses at the scene of an accident. Each witness testifies, "to the best of his knowledge," about what he saw and heard from his own vantage point at the time the incident occurred. That all individuals did *not* perceive the same thing is evidenced by the testimonies of the witnesses for the defense *versus* the witnesses for the prosecution!

Many experiments have demonstrated the phenomenon of optical illusion. Although we rely, to a great extent, on visual sensations for information from the external environment, we often fail to see things as they really are. This frequently happens to us when we participate in sports, particularly those activities that require us to strike an object that is coming toward us, as in tennis or badminton. We may make faulty judgments, based on inaccurate visual perceptions, about where the ball will bounce or where the bird will drop, and therefore we are unable to contact these objects effectively with our racket. Lack of success in this case is due, not to insufficient physical strength, endurance, or flexibility, but to faulty visual perception.

Vision is, of course, not the only modality by which we receive information. We also rely on our hearing for guidance in performance of certain movement patterns. The most clear-cut examples of the use of data gathered from the auditory receptors are to be found in rhythmic activities, such as dance, figure skating to music, synchronized swimming, or any other activity that requires us to coordinate our movements with a superimposed beat or tempo. Not so obvious, but effective nonetheless, is the use of characteristic sound "cues" in a variety of other sports activities. For example, the distinctive sound of a well-hit baseball is a cue to the baseball outfielder that he must race toward the farthest fence if he is going to catch the ball. The difference in the sound of a golf drive hit squarely and the "mushy" sound of a "topped" shot is all too well known to the weekend golfer. Combinations of sight and sound thus provide much information about objects or events experienced in the external environment when we wish to move or are in motion.

Equally important to successful movement activity are the cues that come from our own internal environments when we are in motion. These cues, obtained from the proprioceptors in the muscles and joints of the body (see Chapter 2), tell us the positions of our limbs in space and the directions in which they are moving. The sensations from the proprioceptors, in concert with sensations from the tactile and deep-pressure receptors and the information received from the balance mechanisms housed in the inner ear, enable us to determine where our bodies and body segments are in space. It is this web of evidence, along with auditory sensations, that allows a blind person to play golf, bowl, swim, or do many tasks he wishes to do almost as well as can a sighted person.

The fact is, we often receive far more accurate information from our perceptions of our bodies in motion than we do from our visual perceptions. You may have experienced this yourself at some time when you have been seated in a car that is stopped at a traffic light. You observe a car stopped next to you for the same light and traveling in the same direction as you are. If you look at the car as it is outlined against the buildings across the street, the car you observe is the "object," and the buildings against which it is outlined form the "ground." But if your attention is focused on the interior of your own car and yourself, you and your car become the "objects" and the car next to you becomes the "ground." Thus, when the car next to you begins to move forward slowly, you "perceive" yourself and your own car to be moving slowly backwards, when in fact you are not moving at all. This kind of illusion is so deceptive at times that you must close your eyes and attend to tactile and proprioceptive information to prove to yourself that you are not moving in reverse.

Unfortunately, most of us tend to rely on our visual perceptions to such an extent that we ignore the *feedback* that comes from our proprioceptors and tactile receptors, particularly in the early stages of learning a skill. We give much visual attention to the results of action, e.g., flight of the tennis ball or golf ball, and fail to concentrate on the "feeling" of the motions that propelled these objects.

According to some psychologists who are primarily concerned with the development of human abilities in the young child, movement is essential in early life for the full qualitative development of the perceptions. Through motor activity, movement through space, and exploration of his environment, the young child gathers information that is a precursor to symbolic and logical thought. It is suggested that young children be afforded as many opportunities as possible for moving through space and exploring the environment. Some studies show that children deprived of these movement experiences seem to be more hesitant and fearful of new experiences and have more difficulty in solving problems than children who have had much freedom to explore, test, and refine their perceptual-motor coordination.

Young adults, particularly women, who have not had a rich background of activity experiences throughout childhood and the teens sometimes have difficulty in learning new gross motor skills. This difficulty may be due, to a large extent, to an inability to interpret and make decisions on information from proprioceptive and tactile "feedback." It is not uncommon for women to rely on visual perception and give little attention to data coming from "body sensations" when performing a motor skill unless they have developed the ability to attend to or be conscious of these sensations.

It is the purpose of the experiments at the end of this chapter to help you discover how well *you* attend to a variety of sensory data, and thus to put you on the road to improved motor performance. In some of the experiments you will be blindfolded so that you must rely on perceptions other than visual ones. You will therefore have to attend to information coming to you from auditory, tactile, and proprioceptive sources. In performing such experiments, as well as in learning a new skill in the future, concentrate on the "feeling" and "rhythm" of the motions you make as well as on the results of your movements. You may find that by doing this you will accomplish your goals more quickly.

SUMMARY

1. Various sensory modes give us constant information from both the external and internal environment. The information is received at the receptors and travels over the afferent nerves to the brain. The brain organizes these data, makes a decision based on the meaningful patterns, or *perceptions*, that result, and if a motor response is required it sends out signals to various muscle groups over the efferent nerves.

2. Our visual perceptions of objects and events are not always veridical (true), for they are only what we interpret them to be. Visual perception also sometimes causes us to have illusions that may lead to faulty responses. This is why auditory perception and proprioceptive "feedback" are so important to the successful performance of many movement tasks.

3. Movement through space seems to be a necessity for the development of perceptual ability during the early life of the individual; in adulthood non-veridical perceptions may underlie poor motor performance.

4. Adults, particularly women, tend to rely more on visual perception than "body sensations" for information about motor performance. In learning a new skill, one should attend to tactile and proprioceptive information as well as to visual information to promote successful performance.

SUGGESTED READING

CRATTY, BRYANT J., *Movement Behavior and Motor Learning*. Philadelphia: Lea & Febiger, 1964 (Chapter 13, pp. 256–261)

DEMBER, WILLIAM N., *Psychology of Perception*. New York: Holt, Rinehart and Winston, 1963 (Chapters 5 and 7)

HOCHBERG, JULIAN E., *Perception*. Englewood Cliffs, N.J.: Prentice-Hall, Inc., 1964 (Chapter 5)

EXPERIMENTS IN MOVEMENT AND PERCEPTION

The experiments presented here were designed to give you experiences in attending to nonvisual sensory information that is available to you in a given situation.*

The scoring procedures that are suggested (see Worksheet 5–1) are only a tangible means by which you may assess your performance from trial to trial and from sensory mode to sensory mode. Their purpose is to give you a goal or focus in your attempts to attend to those sensations that will give you the greatest information in each situation.

In most cases it will be easiest to work with a partner, each scoring the other's performance. The scorer should read the scoring directions for each experiment (see Worksheet 5–1) before performance begins.

Experiment 1: Concentration on proprioceptive and auditory information without vision

A. Stand at the foul line on the basketball court, facing the basket.

1) Perform the underhand foul shot three times.

2) Put on a blindfold and perform the underhand foul shot three times.

Questions: Were you able to concentrate on proprioceptive information? Did you use "visual imagery" when you were blindfolded? How do your "sighted" scores compare with your "non-sighted" scores?

B. Repeat the experiment described above, but use the overhand throw of a softball at the wall target which is provided. On the blindfold trials, ask your scorer to tell you after each throw whether you threw the ball above, below, left of, right of, or on the target center.

Experiment 2: Concentration on proprioception and tactile information when vision is distorted

A. In this experiment you will rely on a mirror reflection to trace, in numbered sequence, the dots on a sheet of paper (see Fig. 5–3). You will have a *time limit* of 15 seconds. Grasp a pencil in your preferred hand. Put your hand in the shield-box and look in the mirror. Starting with the dot on the

---

* Some of the experiments require special equipment that will, we hope, be available in the laboratory. Your instructor may choose to substitute appropriate alternative experiments if such equipment is not available.

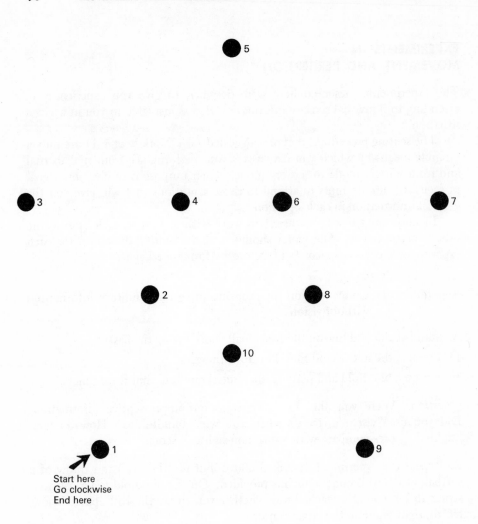

Fig. 5–3. Mirror-tracing pattern (Experiment 2A).

lower left-hand side of the paper, connect all the dots in numerical order by drawing a line between them with your pencil. Move only in a clockwise direction. Have your scorer time you; do not continue beyond 15 seconds.

B. Stand at the start of the straight-line course that is painted on the floor. Look through the "wrong" or large end of the binoculars that are given to you. Attempt to traverse the course in as little time as possible (have scorer time you). Look through the *large end* of the binoculars at all times. Do not remove the binoculars from your eyes until you have reached the end of the course.

Experiment 3: Concentration on auditory information combined with proprioceptive information

A. In this experiment, a small rubber ball will be ejected from a ten-foot tube. Stand on the restraining line painted on the floor with a paddle-tennis racket in your preferred hand (forehand grip). Face the ejector tube. When the ball is ejected attempt to hit it (forehand drive) before it bounces.

1) Perform three trials *without* a blindfold. Concentrate on the "timing" of your striking motion. Do not score these trials.

2) Perform *five* trials while *blindfolded*. Concentrate on the sound of the ball rolling down the tube for the "timing" of your striking motion.

B. In this experiment you are to sit facing an electronic timing device.* Behind a screen is a metronome that is synchronized with the timing device. Press your preferred hand down on the "make contact" button. Listen to the metronome for 10 seconds. Concentrate on the "timing" or tempo of the metronome clicks. Now perform three trials as follows: when you hear the first click of the metronome lift your hand from the "make contact" button and attempt to press the "break contact" button simultaneously with the second click.

Experiment 4: Concentration on tactile and proprioceptive information while moving through space

A. In this experiment you are to go through an obstacle course. Walk through the course once to familiarize yourself with it. Now stand at the starting line, put on your blindfold, and go through the course again while your scorer times you. Have someone who is not blindfolded accompany you as a safety measure.

B. In this experiment your objective is to steer yourself on a straight course, marked by a painted line, while lying on a gym scooter. Give yourself one trial without a blindfold. Lie face down on the gym scooter. Start at the starting line and propelling yourself with your hands, keep the straight line between the wheels of the scooter throughout the entire course. If the wheels touch or cross the line, this counts as an error. Now put your blindfold on and start over from the starting line. Have your scorer time you and count your errors.

---

* If no such timing device is available, set the metronome and attempt to replicate its tempo as described above. No scoring is possible in this case.

WORKSHEET 5-1   Scoresheet for Experiments in Movement and Perception

Experiment 1

A. Scoring for both (1) and (2): 1 point for touching any part of the backboard; 2 points for touching rim or net; 3 points for making a basket. Circle the number that corresponds to the score on each trial:

	Trial 1	Trial 2	Trial 3	Total
1)	1 2 3	1 2 3	1 2 3	_____
2)	1 2 3	1 2 3	1 2 3	_____

B. Scoring for both (1) and (2): 1 point for hitting any part of target but not in a circle or on a line; 3 points for hitting outer circle; 5 points for hitting the next circle; 7 points for hitting center circle. If the ball hits on a line between two circles, award the higher of the two scores.

	Trial 1	Trial 2	Trial 3	Total
1)	1 3 5 7	1 3 5 7	1 3 5 7	_____
2)	1 3 5 7	1 3 5 7	1 3 5 7	_____

Experiment 2

A. Be sure to time the performance (time limit, 15 seconds). Score 5 points for every two dots correctly connected with the pencil line (perfect score = 50 points). From this score, subtract one point for each second taken to perform the task.

Number of pairs of dots connected × 5 = _____ points
Seconds taken to complete task   = _____ points
Net score after subtraction   = _____ points

B. Score one point for each second taken to complete the course. (The lower the score, the better the performance.)

Score: _____ points

WORKSHEET 5-1
(*cont.*)

Experiment 3

A. Score blindfold trials only. Award 5 points for each contact made with the ball by any part of the paddle.

Trial 1 _____ points
Trial 2 _____ points
Trial 3 _____ points
Trial 4 _____ points
Trial 5 _____ points
Total _____ points

B. On each trial, score one point for each $\frac{1}{100}$ second difference between the "break contact" response and the metronome click. (The lower the score, the more accurate the response.)

Trial 1 _____ points
Trial 2 _____ points
Trial 3 _____ points
Total _____ points

Experiment 4

A. Score one point for each second taken to complete the course. (The lower the score, the better the performance.)

Score: _____ points

B. Score one point for each second taken to complete the course. Each time the scooter wheels touch or cross over the line, *add* one penalty point. (The lower the score, the better the performance.)

Seconds taken to complete the course = _____ points
Penalty points for errors   = _____ points
Total score after adding penalty points = _____ points

chapter 6
MOVEMENT AND
AESTHETICS

Movement of the human body has always been a medium for expressing emotions or "feelings" and for communicating ideas. When movements are organized into what we call dance, we have no difficulty in recognizing them as elements of an art form, and therefore as belonging in the realm of aesthetics. But aesthetics, as we shall see, has a relation to many aspects of human endeavor, not just to traditional art forms. In this respect all human movement, for whatever purpose it is performed, is intimately related to aesthetics.

We have chosen to use the spelling of aesthetics in its derivative form rather than the modern version (esthetics) in order to emphasize the fact that the word comes from the Greek *aisthetikos,* which means "perception." Despite the wider meaning that the word has acquired in its English version, perception is still a basic ingredient of aesthetics.

In essence, aesthetics is the philosophy of the beautiful, the science of beauty and "taste." Specifically, aesthetics deals with two major elements that are equal in importance and mutually interactive: the *expression* and the *appreciation* of beauty.

In any discussion of a quality such as beauty, one may get into serious communication difficulties. The reason for this is that objects or events that are perceived as beautiful by one individual may be considered extremely unpleasant and ugly by another individual. Indeed, within each culture and subculture, the standards for what is beauty may differ radically, and in addition, each individual within the culture and subculture has his personal standards or "tastes" by which he evaluates objects or events as "beautiful," "enjoyable," and "exciting."

For example, what judgment might an individual make concerning the aesthetic quality of a symphonic work by Stravinsky, if his previous exposure to music had been limited to the songs of Stephen Foster? Or of an abstract-expressionist painting, if he had never viewed anything but tinted photographs on postcards and calendars? The chances are that he would condemn both the symphony and the painting, since they are strange to his eyes and ears—and yet we know that Stravinsky rates high with musicologists, and that art critics praise the work of many abstract-expressionists.

Our hypothetical individual is not "wrong," however, in liking Foster's songs or postcard art. Aesthetic quality is hardly an "either-or" proposition, but, in fact, exists on a continuum. Thus we cannot say that Stephen Foster's songs are "bad" and symphonic works are "good." Neither can we say that abstract expressionism is "good" and picture postcards and calendars are "bad" (although some of them seem to be pretty far down on the aesthetic scale). We can only say, in each case, that one expression is relatively higher on an aesthetic continuum than is the other.

The fact that it is possible for one object or event to reside higher on a continuum than another implies that there may exist some general principles or criteria that can be applied in assigning relative positions on the scale. Such criteria, or aesthetic principles, do indeed exist, for despite the obvious problems that might arise because of cultural, subcultural, and personal values used in assessing "beauty," certain structural elements seem to be common to all lasting works of art. And through the years, from cave paintings to expressionism, works of art that have been considered to be high on the aesthetic scale have been so evaluated because they have satisfied, to a great degree, certain general aesthetic criteria.

Art Forms and Functional Forms

In our discussion we shall consider art forms to be those products of human endeavor that have had as their primary purpose the expression of an idea or "feeling." Traditionally, such things as sculpture, painting, music, literature, poetry, and classical and modern dance are held to be art forms. These forms of human activity are not intended to be "practical"; rather, they aim to excite emotional response or evoke "ideas" in the viewer or listener. This is not to imply that "practical" products cannot also meet aesthetic criteria or satisfy aesthetic principles. For example, an architect would normally not wish to design a building that was not "functional," or "practical"—his first consideration in design *is* function or practicality. But he may also apply aesthetic criteria or principles to his design. Similarly, the potter may design pots with function or practicality as his prime purpose, but he does not necessarily sacrifice aesthetic principles. And so we can see that the difference between art forms (which are intended first and foremost to meet aesthetic criteria) and functional or practical products (which *may* meet aesthetic criteria) lies in the *purpose* for which they were constructed, not in their relative aesthetic qualities.

AESTHETIC PRINCIPLES AND MOVEMENT ACTIVITIES

Whether an object or activity has been designed to fulfill a practical purpose or an artistic one, the same general principles of aesthetics can be employed to evaluate it. These principles are based on the structural elements of the product and on the organization of these elements.

Lowenfeld* has suggested that the greater the work of art, the less is the possibility of making the slightest change in any of its compositional elements. In such an organization nothing is superfluous—the work represents the highest form of economy, wherein every part is related to the whole and the whole to every part.

The organized compositional elements of any work of art may include such things as line, space, rhythm, accent, contrast, repetition, balance, and color. It seems appropriate to look for these elements in a painting, symphony, piece of sculpture or architecture, even in a piece of pottery, certainly in a dance composition. But it is more difficult to detect the presence of these elements in objects or activities that we usually assess in light of their "practical" outcomes. One of these phenomena is the human in motion.

It is true that dance is recognized as an aesthetic experience for both performer and viewer; but the more "practically oriented" human activities such as games, sports, and daily chores are seldom viewed for their aesthetic qualities. Our limiting perceptual sets seem to keep our attention riveted upon score-points, and prevent us from noticing the beauty of the movement that led to scoring or the prevention of a score. Don't misunderstand—*of course* the end result should be exciting and important! But if we ignore some of the aesthetic pleasure available to us when viewing sports contests, we unwittingly cheat ourselves of a fuller and enriched experience.

Since aesthetics is based on perception, to appreciate the beauty of the human body in motion one must make an effort to "see" the *form* as well as the *function* of movement patterns. By practice, however, the eye may be educated to take in more details of the patterns observed, and thus one's perceptual field is widened and one's discernment heightened.

Even so simple and practical a movement as walking randomly from "here" to "there" may be a pleasure to observe (depending on the movement organization of the walker). A correspondingly greater pleasure is yielded by observation of well-executed movements that are sparked by drive or purpose. For example, a long completed touchdown pass becomes an even greater thrill to watch if one is aware of the beautiful rhythm and timing of the quarterback as he throws, the organizational unity of the receiver as he leaps high to catch the ball, and the forceful accent and spacing of the blockers as they carry out their assignments. Similar examples could be offered in

---

* See Viktor Lowenfeld, *Creative and Mental Growth*. New York: Macmillan, 1957.

almost any sport. Attention to the beauty of line, balance, rhythm, accent, and economy of effort displayed by a great tennis player as he serves a tennis ball, to the space-time-force organization of a good·golf swing, to the graceful, disciplined movements of the gifted gymnast, swimmer, diver, pole-vaulter, runner, or javelin- and discus-thrower—such attention can make one's enjoyment and appreciation of any of these events a fuller aesthetic experience. The fact that the traditional measures of the quality of these events are minutes, seconds, feet, inches, and points should not distract us from an appreciation of the beauty of the movements themselves.

Inner Aisthetikos

Thus far we have discussed movement and aesthetics only in relation to observations of the performance of others. But a great deal of aesthetic pleasure may be derived from our own movement experiences. As we have described in another chapter, through proprioception we receive a constant supply of "feedback" sensations from our own unique organization of movement. Perception of our movements is tactile-kinesthetic rather than visual. The farther up on the aesthetic continuum is our organization of the elements of the movement pattern we are performing, the more unity of "feeling" we receive from our own motions and the more pleasurable is the experience. Whether we organize our movements for the purpose of performing a *tour jeté* or for the purpose of driving a golf ball, if the movements involved are high on the scale of "economy" and if ". . . every part is related to the whole and the whole to every part,"* then we experience the pleasure of "just rightness." The more proficient we become the more frequently do we experience these "feelings" of unity.

To describe aesthetic experiences in verbal symbols is a difficult task—indeed, perhaps the attempt is hopeless, because the "feelings" and "meanings" involved are personal matters that must fall within one's own experiencing before understanding can come about. Our hope is that you will increasingly attend to those sensations that arise from your own organization of movement patterns, so that as you increase in your proficiency to perform whatever movement task you choose to do, you may heighten the enjoyment you derive from your performance.

SUMMARY

1. The word *aesthetics* comes from the Greek word *aisthetikos*, meaning "perception." Aesthetics deals with the two mutually interacting elements, the *expression* and the *appreciation* of beauty. It is the *science* of "beauty," the *philosophy* of the "beautiful."

---

* See Viktor Lowenfeld, *Creative and Mental Growth*. New York: Macmillan, 1957.

2. Although there are cultural, subcultural, and personal standards for what is aesthetically pleasing or enjoyable, certain structural elements and their organization seem to be common to all objects or events that have, over long periods of time, been considered high on the aesthetic scale or continuum.

3. Some of the structural elements involved in the organization of aesthetic products are line, space, rhythm, accent, contrast, repetition, balance, and color. The higher on the aesthetic scale a product is, the more economical and unified is the organization of structural elements.

4. Since aesthetics is based on perception, one's appreciation of the form and function of movement of the human body (one's own proprioceptively perceived performance as well as the visually perceived performance of others) is dependent on an "educating" of the sensorium to produce a widening of one's perceptual field and a heightening of one's discernment.

SUGGESTED READING

Kepes, Gyorgy (ed.), *Education of Vision*. New York: George Braziller, 1965

Langer, Susanne, *Philosophy in a New Key*. New York: Mentor Books, 1955

Lowenfeld, Viktor, *Creative and Mental Growth*. New York: Macmillan Company, 1957

Smith, Hope M., "Creative expression and physical education." *Journal of Health, Physical Education and Recreation* 33, 38–39 (1962)

EXPERIMENTS IN MOVEMENT AND AESTHETICS

The following experiences are designed to help you experiment with organizing your own movement patterns into aesthetic products. In Part A of the experiment you will try to attend to a musical stimulus and respond to this stimulus by recording your response on a large piece of newsprint with colored chalks. Part B of the experiment outlines the ways in which you can organize a series of movement patterns into a unified expression of your own graphic response to the initial musical stimulus.

Part A

Equipment: A sheet of newsprint (large), a box of colored chalks, a record player, and a recording of some symphonic work, e.g., Beethoven's *Eroica*, or Dvorak's *D Minor*.

Directions: Place the newsprint on the floor. Sit or kneel on the floor with the newsprint in front of you. Select a dark piece of chalk, preferably black, with which you can record your response to the music. When your instructor starts the music, listen to it for a few bars and get the "feeling" of the rhythm and tempo. It may help you to concentrate on the sounds if you close your eyes as you listen.

When you have your impression of the music well in mind place your chalk anywhere on the piece of newsprint and start to move it over the paper in response to the music. Use large movements of your arm and do not lift the chalk from the paper. Use *all* of the paper for your design. Attend to the rhythm, tempo, contrast, and accents in the music.

When you have covered your paper with what you consider to be enough "thematic lines and spaces," continue listening to the music and begin to select spaces and lines on your graphic recording which you will organize into a unity of expression. Fill in the spaces you select with your choice of colors so that you begin to delineate shapes and forms related to one another and to the whole.

When you have completed your "product" you will have a visualized expression of your auditory and kinesthetic impressions of the music. Remember that the finished work does not need to be a "representational" expression of familiar objects, such as faces, houses, flowers, and so forth. As a matter of fact, it will probably be more effective if it is an abstract expression.

Part B

Using your own graphic expression of the music as the stimulus, devise a series of movements that will express the line, space, rhythm, accent, color, and thematic qualities of your own work. Organize these movements into a unity that you feel most clearly depicts what you have organized on paper.

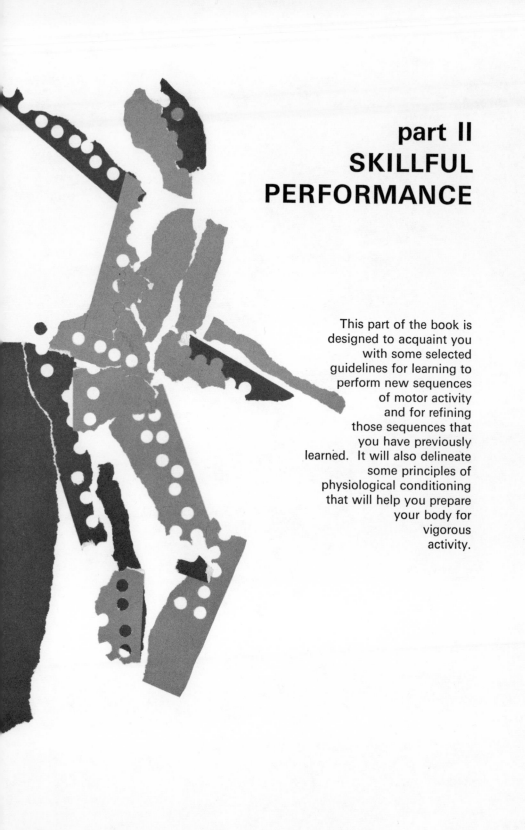

part II
SKILLFUL PERFORMANCE

This part of the book is
designed to acquaint you
with some selected
guidelines for learning to
perform new sequences
of motor activity
and for refining
those sequences that
you have previously
learned. It will also delineate
some principles of
physiological conditioning
that will help you prepare
your body for
vigorous
activity.

chapter 7
LEARNING TO MOVE
SKILLFULLY

In Part I of this book you have been reading about why humans move as they do. You have examined the nature of human movement, the range of movement possibilities as dictated by human structure and function, and the physical laws that affect human movement. You have read that movement is a nonverbal "language" that operates as a medium for communication in a culture, and that individual movement behavior is greatly influenced by the culture in which one is raised. And you have explored the complexity of the human sensation-perception system and its integral relationship to movement behavior.

These topics represent the broad parameters of human movement. But as has already been emphasized, all humans do not move alike. Starting from essentially the same basic "raw materials," each person develops his own unique movement behavior. What, then, is the principal influence in changing these *common* "raw materials" of human movement into the *individualized* "finished products" which each person exhibits? The answer lies primarily in the phenomenon of *learning*.

With respect to the development of your own unique movement behavior:

1) You *learn* what your own capabilities and limitations for movement are relative to your specific structural characteristics.

2) You *learn* to increase your capabilities for movement experiences by increasing the efficiency of certain physiological functions.

3) You *learn* to deal with the physical laws such as gravity, which affect your movement behavior constantly.

4) You *learn* movement qualities and specific characteristics from the familial and cultural setting in which you mature.

5) You *learn* to use your sense modalities for perceiving the world around you. You *learn* patterns of perceptual organization which trigger the movement behavior you exhibit.

Your movement behavior is, therefore, the product of an interaction between the "raw materials" of your hereditary and species characteristics on the one hand, and the total environment in which you live, on the other. These raw materials are molded into finished movement behavior products primarily through learning.

It is the purpose of this chapter to examine learning and the learning process carefully, so that you may develop some effective techniques for enhancing your own movement behavior in general, and so that you may become a more effective, self-directed learner of specific sport, game, or dance skills which may interest you.

BASIC ABILITIES VERSUS MOTOR SKILLS

Before embarking on a discussion of how one learns specific movement *skills*, it seems appropriate to distinguish between the terms "ability" and "skill." Fleishman* has said that ". . . ability refers to a more general trait of the individual," and that abilities, as contrasted with skills, ". . . are fairly enduring traits, which in the adult, are more difficult to change." He suggests that many abilities are a product of learning, while a few are a result of inheritance; but, by and large, basic abilities are a result of the combination of both. For our purposes, let us think of an "ability" as a quality or trait that you bring with you as you attempt to learn a new task. Let us think of a "skill" as a highly specific movement sequence related to the accomplishment of a single task. Some examples of abilities are reaction time and manual dexterity. Examples of skills are basketball shooting or a tennis forehand.

The primary reason for making this distinction is to help you answer the question, "Am I capable of learning the series of complex movement skills involved in such games as golf or tennis?" Some of you may perceive yourselves as "uncoordinated" or "not athletic"—you feel that you cannot develop motor skillfulness to any satisfying level of proficiency. But this is definitely not the case.

Certainly, there are some hereditary or constitutional limits beyond which no person can hope to go. But these limits are rarely, if ever, reached. Not too many years ago, for example, it was thought that a man was incapable of running a mile in less than four minutes. The sub-four-minute mile is achieved rather regularly now by several athletes, and the great Jim Ryun of Kansas is pointing toward a 3:50 mile. This is an extreme example, since most of us do not fall into the same category as the Jim Ryuns of the world. Nevertheless, research evidence has shown, on many occasions, that *the most*

---

* See Edwin A. Fleishman, "Human abilities and the acquisition of skills," in *Acquisition of Skill*, edited by Edward A. Bilodeau. New York: Academic Press, 1966.

critical factors operating to produce motor skillfulness seem to be *motivational* and *experiential*, rather than physical, in nature.

Statistical analyses have proved that there are no such qualities as *general* "athletic" or "motor" ability. Therefore, you have no basis for concluding that you are "uncoordinated" or a "motor moron." The requirements for skillfulness, in any given large-muscle activity, seem to be highly specific. Certain minimum amounts of the elements of organic fitness—i.e., strength, endurance, and flexibility—are required to perform any skill, but these can be developed or improved at will (see Chapter 8). Even those of you who begin the learning of a specific motor skill with high levels of proficiency in certain "basic abilities" can increase those levels through learning.

The major point to remember when learning motor skills is that persons who possess the *desire* and *persistence* to learn specific skills, do so. Evidence clearly indicates that people learn what they *want* to learn, and that they tend to continue to engage in activities in which they are relatively proficient, and from which they derive personal satisfaction.

With the above discussion in mind let us proceed to explore in more detail how one learns to move skillfully.

THE CONCEPT OF LEARNING

It has been said that living, moving, and behaving are almost synonymous terms. You may have encountered the phrase "learning is behaving" in a general psychology textbook. You have been engaged in this process of learning ever since you can remember, whether or not you identified it as such. Some of the earliest and most basic behaviors partially due to learning are essentially "motor" in nature, i.e., walking, climbing, reaching, and grasping. Even the development of language is fundamentally a motor task, since it involves complex coordination of the muscles of the face, lips, tongue, throat, and thorax. Some of us even "talk" with our hands.

The question arises as to whether there is a basic difference between learning to manipulate the body (sometimes called motor learning), and learning to manipulate verbal symbols and ideas (sometimes called verbal or concept learning). Think of the highly successful quarterback who must select and execute any number of complicated football plays during a game. It would be erroneous to imply that he is not "cerebrating" during the entire game. Thus we can see that "motor learning" is a very restrictive and arbitrary term. Evidence supports the conclusion that *learning* is *learning* regardless of the form it takes or the products which accrue from it—all learning requires some general processes, whether one is learning abstract mathematical concepts or learning to hit a tennis ball, and all learning requires *thinking* and *concentration* if it is to be productive.

Gregory A. Kimble, a noted psychologist, has defined learning as "a relatively permanent change in behavioral potentiality which occurs as the result of reinforced practice."* Let us examine this statement carefully with the view toward converting the abstract terminology into real or operational examples.

The first phrase, "a relatively permanent change in behavioral potentiality," should communicate to you one fundamental concept, namely, that we can only *infer* that learning has occurred in a given situation by observing overt changes in behavior. What actually happens within the human organism when learning takes place is not completely understood. For example, the only way anyone can be sure that you have learned the skill of reading is to observe your reading behavior. He may listen to you as you read aloud, or ask you questions about some material you have read. Similarly, the only way anyone can be sure that you have learned to swim is to observe your swimming behavior. The learning *process* occurs within the organism, and cannot be observed or measured directly; the *products* of learning, i.e., skillfulness in reading or swimming, are manifested in overt behavior and can be observed and measured directly. From the assessment of these products we can infer or *indirectly assume* that the process of learning has taken place.

The second phrase in Kimble's definition of learning, "which occurs as a result of reinforced practice," sorts out behavioral changes that may be due to fatigue, maturation, or changes in motivational state from those that are due to learning. For example, if we look at a child's running behavior at age two and again at age five, we find marked differences. This change of behavior over time in performing the basic movement sequence of running is due mainly to growth and maturational changes. Similarly, your tennis-playing behavior may be better on a bright sunny morning, after a good night's sleep, than it is in the afternoon, after you have had a long and busy day at school. The difference in the latter case may be due primarily to fatigue or lack of motivation. You have not "forgotten" how to play tennis.

The definition of learning presented above is couched in abstract terms, but it is possible to restate it in operational terms for any specific task or skill that you may wish to learn. As you attempt to learn movement skills you should try to define operationally, what you are attempting to learn in order to help you assess your own progress toward behavioral goals.

THE CONCEPT OF SKILL

The terms "skill," "skilled," "skillful," "skillfulness," etc., as used in our language, have several different connotations. For purposes of this book about

---

* Gregory A. Kimble, "Categories of learning and the problem of definition," in *Categories of Human Learning*, edited by Arthur W. Melton. New York: Academic Press, 1964.

human movement it seems important to examine the various interpretations in some detail.

Earlier in this chapter we defined skill as "a highly specific movement sequence related to the accomplishment of a single task." Let us test certain common uses of the word "skill" to see if they do indeed fulfill this particular definition.

The term "skill" has been applied to such basic movement sequences as running, jumping, and throwing. This seems an inappropriate use of the term, since these basic sequences develop in the formative years mainly as a result of maturation. On the other hand, when these basic sequences are utilized with some *specific* goal in view, such as running the 100-yard dash, performing the standing broad jump, or throwing the discus, then additional responses must be learned that are specific to the task, and any of these more complex movement tasks may accurately be termed a skill.

"Skill" has also been used to refer to a whole collection of movement responses that are goal-directed; for example, some people refer to the "skill" of golf or swimming or dancing. This use of the term is also inaccurate, since any one of these activities obviously involves the learning of many independent movement and judgment responses, rather than just a single task as our definition prescribes.

Examples of tasks which do fulfill our definition are: the breast stroke in swimming, a jack-knife dive, a forehand drive in tennis, the polka step in folk dancing, the underhand serve in volleyball, putting in golf, and so forth. These activities all involve "highly specific movement sequences related to the accomplishment of a single task."

In order to provide a common understanding and frame of reference we must make two additional terminology distinctions. In this chapter we shall *not* use the term "skill" as a synonym for proficiency in performance—we shall restrict its use to the movement sequences themselves. Furthermore, we shall avoid the use of "skillful" or "skillfulness" as absolutes, referring to highly proficient performance only. Skill learning exists on a continuum; there are many degrees of proficiency in any task. Thus one is neither "skillful" nor "unskillful" at any task; one merely possesses *less* or *more* skillfulness at any point in time. It is through the process of learning that one increases his level of proficiency.

Now that we have laid some foundation understandings about the learning process and movement skills we can proceed to examine more specifically how one learns to move skillfully. The following discussion focuses on the kinds of things it would be helpful for you to know and put into practice when you tackle such formidable tasks as the learning of golf, basketball, badminton, or any other movement form. It should help you become aware of the complexity of learning movement skills and assist you in improving your movement behavior.

FACTORS AFFECTING THE ACQUISITION OF SKILLS

Preparatory set. One of the most important first steps one must take when attempting to learn a new skill is to develop a *preparatory set* to learn. *Set* may be described as an expectancy, a readiness, or a preparedness to attend to the relevant sensory information that will be forthcoming in a new learning situation.

Your expectancies can be influenced by prior experiences as well as present elements in the environment. For example, in Chapter 10 we shall suggest ways to explore some of the mechanical and perceptual principles of human movement in the aquatic medium. Now, your preparatory set when entering a "swimming class" is geared toward acquiring skillfulness in swimming. You might ask yourself, "What good will it do me to know about something called a center of buoyancy? I want to learn to swim." Your expectancy or preparatory set has been influenced by your prior experiences with more conventional physical education classes or swimming lessons. To benefit from the material in Chapter 10, you will have to overcome a prior perceptual set and establish a new one.

Motivation. It is generally recognized that you will learn only what you are motivated to learn. Motivation functions as the energizer that initiates, sustains, and improves human performance. Time and again it has been found that human performance is usually heightened by increases in motivation and lessened by decreases in motivation. Gagné and Fleishman suggest that motivation interacts with the level of skillfulness to affect performance to a dramatic degree. They state, ". . . there is much evidence to make us think that motivation does not simply *add* to skill in producing performance, but rather *multiplies* with it."*

Lack of motivation, of course, means no performance at all. Human motives are complex, varied, and highly personal. They are affected and effected by physiological, psychological, and cultural considerations. You may want to learn to swim for a number of reasons, i.e., it may be a popular activity among your friends (a social motive); it can provide vigorous physical activity (a physiological motive); it is an activity that you cannot now perform (curiosity or achievement motive), and so on. But if swimming is something you "couldn't care less" about, you most assuredly will not learn a great deal even if you are required to take a swimming course.

Let us assume now that you *are* motivated to learn some motor activity and that you have established a preparatory set to learn. What further specific factors will affect your progress toward skill development?

---

* Robert M. Gagné and Edwin A. Fleishman, *Psychology and Human Performance.* New York: Holt, Rinehart and Winston, 1959.

Role of Practice and Information about Performance

There is no condition of greater importance in the development of a motor skill than practice. Practice means, not merely going through the motions, but repeating the desired response sequences with *reinforcement for correct performance*. Reinforcement may be in terms of a tangible reward (the ball went in the basket), an intangible reward (the cartwheel felt right), an extrinsic reward (your boyfriend complimented you on your golf swing), or an intrinsic reward (you finally executed that dance step just the way you wanted to). Note that the rewards in all these cases depend on awareness of results, not just on the motions in themselves.

Thus the old cliché "practice makes perfect" is not quite accurate. It is not practice *alone* which leads to perfection, but *effective* practice. How, then, can one judge the effectiveness of practice?

Concurrent sensory feedback. The most immediate source of information about effectiveness of practice is *sensory feedback*. Learning a motor skill is closely associated with sensory acuity and power of perception (recall Chapter 5). The learner is bombarded with sensory information during the performance of a movement task: visual, auditory, and tactile stimuli from the environment in addition to proprioceptive sensations from within one's own body. Some of the stimuli may be relevant and others irrelevant to the task at hand. Some may be attended to, others ignored. Perhaps the most difficult task of the beginner is to sort out the relevant from the irrelevant stimuli: to attend to important, and reject extraneous, sensory information.

Think of yourself as a novice golfer so that we may illustrate the role of sensory feedback in learning. The only goal that you, the prospective golfer, may have in mind is hitting the ball—a goal that seems relatively simple on the surface. But let us take a closer look at the myriad sensory data impinging on you as you prepare to accomplish your goal. You *look* at the ball and then judge how far to stand from it, judge the length of your club, and determine the direction in which you wish to hit the ball. You *look* at your hands to check your grip, and perhaps align the club head with the ball repeatedly. You *feel* the club in your hands and the distribution of your weight on the soles of your feet. When you move you become aware, by *looking* and *feeling*, of the direction and speed of your movements as well as the relative position of your body segments at some point in the swing. If you hit the ball you *hear* the blow of the club face as it contacts the ball; if you miss it there is an obvious absence of this auditory input.

All of the above are examples of *concurrent sensory feedback* that can provide you with potentially useful information about your performance. Now, evidence seems to indicate that in the *initial* stages of learning a new motor task, visual feedback is the most informative and useful. It plays a regulatory role particularly with respect to providing error information. As performance becomes habitual and skillfulness increases, however, internal proprioceptive feedback becomes increasingly important. The moment he hits the ball, the championship golfer knows whether it will be a 250-yard drive down the middle of the fairway or a hook into the rough, simply by the way the swing and impact felt.

There is an important functional relationship between sensory feedback and practice. As practice continues and skills become more refined, the performer's responses become automatized. Less conscious attention has to be directed toward the details of bodily movement. It is easier to detect errors. Output more nearly meets the demands imposed by input. Internal feedback is more dependable and one is free to concentrate on the subtleties of the performance.

Initial learning of a motor task involves concentration on *stimulus discrimination*, while refinement of performance involves gradual *response modification*. Research evidence clearly shows that improvement of motor skill can continue over long periods of time, even several years. What seem to be plateaus in performance are more likely to be traceable to changes in motivation or temporary fatigue rather than to attainment of one's performance capacity.

Knowledge of results. In addition to concurrent sensory feedback, there is another important type of information about the effectiveness of practice. This is the information the performer receives after a performance is completed. Some psychologists refer to this as "terminal feedback." We shall simply call it *knowledge of results.* The performer may perceive this information for himself (as in seeing the arrow hit the target) or he may have it relayed to him from some outside source (as in being told that he ran the 60-yard dash in seven seconds or threw a softball 140 feet).

Knowledge of results plays an important role in learning, for it assists a performer in setting realistic goals for skill achievement. Practice, to be effective, must be purposeful and goal-oriented. In the initial stages of learning the teacher may have to take a direct role in goal-setting, but as learning proceeds and skillfulness increases, the learner should set his own goals so that he becomes increasingly independent of the teacher or coach. Note that goals should be realistic—difficult enough to be challenging, but not so difficult that one becomes discouraged. The more specific the knowledge of results can be, the more rapidly skill development can proceed.

An example. Let us now examine the interrelationships among concurrent feedback, goal-setting, and knowledge of results in the learning of a particular skill. We shall use the skill of rolling a bowling ball as the example.

In order to knock down all of the pins at one time the ball must be thrown with at least a minimum amount of velocity. The throwing pattern utilized in bowling is the underarm swing pattern. The first goal then becomes performance of this swing to achieve a predetermined standard of velocity in delivery of the ball.

The pins are removed from the end of the alley (since they are an extraneous visual cue at this point in skill development), and the performer is left free to practice the swing and delivery alone. She is told to concentrate on the feel of the swing, its speed and direction, and the weight of the ball (examples of concurrent feedback). After the performance is completed she is told by the instructor what the ball-speed was from release to pin receptacle on each delivery (knowledge of results).

The performer continues to practice until the speed goal is reached quite consistently, indicating that the correct response sequence has become relatively automatic. Then a new and more difficult goal is set. Perhaps the #1 and #3 pins are placed on the alley and the goal becomes one of accuracy. Learning and improvement continue in a similar manner until the more general goal of learning to bowl is attained with a reasonable degree of success and satisfaction.

By the method of progressive goal-setting and diligent practice with attention to feedback and knowledge of results, skill learning proceeds and performance improves continuously. If the outcomes of motor responses cannot be observed, no learning takes place. Practice without knowledge of results is a waste of time and effort.

Length and Distribution of Practice. Practice that is continuous and concentrated over a long period of time is referred to as *massed practice.* A situation providing more frequent pauses or rest periods is spoken of as *spaced* or *distributed practice.* Suppose, now, that you have allotted yourself eight hours for the practice of your forehand drive in tennis. Should you practice one hour a day for eight days or practice for eight hours in one day? In the massed-practice period two factors would seem to influence the effectiveness of practice—fatigue and decreased motivation. It is unlikely that you would be able to sustain your physical output or your interest in the practice over such a long period of time. This is particularly true in the initial stages of skill learning. The expert tennis player might benefit from massed practice. But, in general, distributed practice has been shown to be more effective in skill learning than massed practice.

RETENTION OF MOTOR SKILLS

Motor skills, once learned, seem to be better retained over long periods of time than other types of skills. For example, you may have forgotten most of the French vocabulary that you learned in junior high school, but you can probably roller-skate or ride a bicycle with some degree of proficiency even if you have not done so for years. The primary reason for this high degree of retention is that motor skills are usually *overlearned*—that is, the skill is repeated so often that it becomes automatic. Because one may overlearn incorrect as well as correct skill responses, it is imperative that efficient response sequences be learned initially.

The *degree* to which one retains proficiency in a motor skill is a function of how well one learned the skill originally. A greater proportion of skillfulness is lost when smaller amounts of initial practice have been given. Also, the longer a skill has been unpracticed the greater the proportion of skillfulness that may be lost. The once-successful tournament golfer who has not played in years cannot expect to shoot a round in par the first time out, but a relatively short period of practice may restore her game to its prior level of proficiency.

TRANSFER OF LEARNING

Does being highly skillful in one movement task assist in learning a new one? All learning is based on the general notion that the outcomes or products will be useful in a variety of working situations. If one were always to have to "start from scratch," so to speak, when attempting to learn a new task, then the repertoire of human skills would be limited indeed.

The degree to which the learning of one skill facilitates—or interferes with—the learning of a new one has been called transfer of learning. If skillfulness in one task *facilitates* the learning of a new one, *positive transfer* is said to have occurred. Skillfulness in one task may sometimes interfere with the learning of a new one; in this case *negative transfer* is said to have occurred.

As a general rule, when you have learned one motor skill, the learning of a new but similar one will usually be easier and faster. The critical condition for positive transfer or facilitation is the degree of similarity of the two tasks.

Evidence seems to show that the most dependable condition for high positive transfer is *stimulus similarity*. For example, the golfer might practice putting on a putting green before playing a round of golf. The stimulus characteristics encountered during the practice are very similar to those which will be present on the greens of the golf course. One would expect high positive transfer to occur between these two situations. If the same golfer practiced her putting *only* at home on the livingroom rug, using a drinking-glass placed on its side for the cup, one could not expect the same amount of positive transfer to occur. In this situation many of the stimulus characteristics are dissimilar. The surface of the rug is very different from the grassy surface of the green. The stimuli from the surrounding visual field are quite different. The drinking-glass target is in a different spatial orientation than a cup would be on a putting green. These dissimilarities, as well as others, would reduce the amount of positive transfer between the two situations.

Another condition that assists in positive transfer of learning is the similarity of the response elements (or response sequences) in two tasks. In general, the more nearly identical the two tasks are, the more one can expect that being skillful in the first task will facilitate learning a new but similar one. For example, if you learned first to drive a car with an automatic gear shift, the control for which was on the steering column, you would probably have a little difficulty in adjusting to one with an automatic transmission that was controlled by pushbuttons. The pushbuttons require a subskill for shifting that is not needed for the operation of a car with automatic transmission controls on the steering column. However, all other responses required to drive the two kinds of cars are practically identical. In this respect, learning the first task has facilitated to a high degree the learning of the second.

It was mentioned earlier that negative transfer, or interference, can occur between two tasks. In learning sports skills this can occur in situations where one might expect positive transfer to occur upon cursory examination of the requirements of two sports. Let us take the example of the highly skillful tennis player who wishes to learn to play badminton, and see just how similar these two movement experiences are. Each sport involves similar responses or habits in the form of basic movement sequences—the overarm and sidearm swing patterns, and running. The two sports are quite different, however, in the stimuli involved: The flight of the tennis ball is quite different in speed and trajectory from the flight of the badminton bird; the racket weights and lengths are different; and the courts are quite unlike one another in size and net-height. Therefore certain automatic response sequences learned in tennis might interfere with skill development in badminton. The interference might not persist, but the tennis player might take longer to become skillful in badminton than she would if she had never learned to play tennis.

As a general rule, increasing similarity of tasks, either in stimulus similarity or response similarity, leads to increasing amounts of positive transfer or facilitation from one task to a new task. As tasks decrease in similarity, less positive transfer is likely and a condition of zero or negative transfer may result.

SUMMARY

1. Your movement behavior is the product of both the "raw materials" of your hereditary and species characteristics and your interaction with the total environment in which you live. How these raw materials are molded into the finished movement behavior products is due primarily to learning.

2. A *basic ability* is a general trait, such as manual dexterity, that is fairly enduring in an individual. A *skill* is a highly specific movement sequence related to the accomplishment of a single task, such as a fancy dive. There

is no such thing as a "motor moron" in the medically normal population. The most critical factors operating to produce motor skillfulness seem to be *motivational* and *experiential* in nature. Persons who possess the *desire* and *persistence* to learn specific skills do so.

3. Evidence supports that *learning* is *learning* regardless of the form it takes or the products that accrue from it. All learning requires the same general processes. Learning is defined as "a relatively permanent change in behavioral potentiality which occurs as the result of reinforced practice."* We cannot observe the learning process directly; that learning has occurred must be *inferred* from observing overt behavioral changes.

4. In this text the terms "skillful" or "skillfulness" are used to refer to the level of proficiency which one has acquired in the performance of a "skill." Skillfulness is on a continuum, and may be increased through learning.

5. Certain factors are important in the acquisition of skills. *Preparatory set* is described as an expectancy, readiness, or preparedness to learn. Set can be affected by prior experiences. *Motivation* functions as an energizer which initiates, sustains, and improves human performance.

6. There is no condition of greater importance in the development of a motor skill than *practice*. It is not practice *per se* that leads to perfection, but *effective* practice. Information about effectiveness of practice can be gained in two ways: *concurrent sensory feedback* during performance, and *knowledge of results* after the performance has been completed.

7. Initial learning of a motor task involves essentially *stimulus discrimination*, while refinement of performance involves gradual *response modification*.

8. Practice, to be effective, must be purposeful and *goal-oriented*. Goals should be realistic—difficult enough to be challenging, but not so difficult that one becomes discouraged. As learning proceeds, the learner should try to set her own goals so as to become independent of the teacher.

9. When practice is continuous or concentrated over a long period of time, it is called *massed practice*. A situation providing more frequent pauses or rest periods is called *spaced* or *distributed practice*. In general, distributed practice has been shown to be more effective in the learning of a skill than massed practice.

10. Motor skills, once learned, seem to be better retained over long periods of time than other types of skills. The primary reason for this high degree of retention is that motor skills are usually *overlearned*.

---

* Gregory W. Kimble, "Categories of learning and the problem of definition," in *Categories of Human Learning*, edited by Arthur W. Melton. New York: Academic Press, 1964.

11. The degree to which the learning of one skill facilitates or interferes with the learning of a new one has been called *transfer of learning*. As a general rule, when you have learned one motor skill, the learning of a new but similar one will usually be easier and faster. Evidence seems to show that the most dependable condition for high positive transfer is *stimulus similarity*. Also, the more nearly identical the response sequences are in two tasks, the more positive transfer can be expected to occur from the first task to a new one. As tasks decrease in similarity, less positive transfer is likely and a condition of zero or negative transfer may result.

SUGGESTED READING

GAGNÉ, ROBERT M., AND EDWIN A. FLEISHMAN, *Psychology and Human Performance*. New York: Holt, Rinehart and Winston, 1959 (Chapters 6 and 8)

KNAPP, BARBARA, *Skill in Sport*. London: Routledge and Kegan Paul, 1963 (Chapters III, IV, and VI)

MCKEACHIE, WILBERT J., AND CHARLOTTE L. DOYLE, *Psychology*. Reading, Mass.: Addison-Wesley Publishing Co., Inc., 1966 (Chapters 5, 7, and 8)

chapter 8
CONDITIONING

The performance of any movement task requires a certain level of physiological fitness. The tasks of daily life, such as walking, lifting, and carrying, each make certain demands on the musculoskeletal, circulatory, and respiratory systems of the body. And although a single performance of such tasks may require only a minimum level of physiological fitness, a much higher level may be required to engage in a task over a period of time without feeling fatigued.

A process that prepares an individual to engage in movement tasks with physiological efficiency is called *conditioning*. This term, as it is being used here, does not refer to the training and practice of the movement tasks themselves, but rather to the development of specific physiological qualities that are essential for achieving certain levels of skillfulness in a movement task and for being able to continue in the task over a relatively long period of time.

Although conditioning in its broadest sense embraces the development of all aspects of an individual's readiness for action, the discussion in this chapter is limited to three physiological qualities that appear to be necessary prerequisites for achieving success in most movement situations. These three qualities are (a) strength and endurance of the skeletal muscles, (b) cardiovascular-respiratory endurance, and (c) flexibility. The development of a minimum level of all these qualities is considered desirable for general health; in addition, each movement task makes specific physiological demands on the individual.

For example, arm and shoulder strength may be extremely important in some movement situations but relatively unimportant in other situations. A certain level of cardiovascular-respiratory endurance is essential in order to play several sets of tennis, but this quality is relatively unimportant in bowling. Bowling, in its turn, requires a certain level of finger grip strength in order to maintain a firm grip on the ball during the arc of the swing. A recent comparison of relatively high-level and low-level performers in gymnastic activities revealed that the high-level performers had greater flexibility of the lower back and posterior thigh muscles; they were able to project the body to a greater height in a vertical direction, and they could move the body segments as well as the total body more rapidly. Although cause and effect relationships cannot be established on the basis of these findings, there is at least logical validity in suggesting that certain levels of strength and flexibility are requisite to performance in gymnastic activities.

In order to achieve at least a minimum level of skill in a given task, then, it would seem desirable to consider the physiological demands of the task and then to compare one's own level of physiological fitness in relation to those demands. The purpose of this chapter is to examine the *nature* of strength and muscular endurance, cardiovascular-respiratory endurance, and flexibility and to identify the *principles* related to the development of these specific qualities.

THE NATURE OF STRENGTH AND MUSCULAR ENDURANCE

Movement of the body and body parts is made possible by the contraction of skeletal muscles. In performing various movement tasks, it is important that each muscle be able to contract with varying degrees of strength. This is accomplished by summing the contractions of varying numbers of muscle fibers at once. In general, it has been found that the gradations of muscular contractions depend on (a) the number of motor units in action and (b) the frequency of response of each individual unit.

Until recently, it was thought that strength development was dependent only on physiological changes in the muscle tissues. There is now evidence that the ability of the muscle to overcome progressively heavier loads is also influenced by learning and the formation of neuromuscular patterns.

Before we proceed any further, let us define what we mean by "strength." Depending on how the term is used, different operational definitions appear in the literature. To some writers strength means the *amount of tension* that can be exerted in *a single maximum contraction*. Others define strength as the ability of the muscle to contract against *submaximal resistance for a long period of time*. The first definition is valid when one is interested in the maximum strength limits of the individual; the second definition applies to that quality usually referred to as muscular endurance rather than strength. There is some evidence to suggest, however, that strength and muscular endurance are a part of the same continuum. At one end of the continuum is a single contraction against maximum resistance. At the other end of the continuum is a maximum number of contractions against a submaximal resistance. If an individual is concerned with increasing the ability to work against greater resistance, such as supporting the body in gymnastic skills, then conditioning procedures which require a limited number of maximum contractions would appear to be desirable. If, on the other hand, an individual wishes to engage in an activity such as long-distance swimming, conditioning procedures should involve doing a number of repetitions against a submaximal resistance.

Comparative studies of isometric exercises (in which the muscle used remains essentially the same length) and isotonic exercises (in which the muscle changes in length), tend to indicate that isometric exercises are the more effective for increasing maximum strength limits.

Principles of Strength Development

Whether a program is based on isometric or isotonic training methods, the available research evidence indicates that an increase in muscle strength depends on an increase in tension over that previously exerted. This is known as the "overload" principle and is the dominating factor in strength development. As strength increases, the load against which the muscle is exerting force must be constantly increased in order to assure continued improvement. There is general agreement in the literature that an increase in strength will result by applying the overload principle in the following ways:

1) gradually increasing the resistance, or

2) with a constant resistance, gradually increasing the total number of repetitions.

The first method is recommended for increasing the amount of tension that can be exerted in a single contraction; the second method is recommended for increasing the ability to continue submaximal contractions over a long period of time. Gradations of resistance and/or repetitions, of course, can be used for developing strength levels to meet the demands of specific movement tasks.

THE NATURE OF
CARDIOVASCULAR-RESPIRATORY ENDURANCE

As early as 1884, an Italian by the name of Mosso experimented with the effects of exercising a muscle on an ergometer (an apparatus for measuring the work capacity of a muscle). Mosso was one of the first physiologists to hypothesize that muscular efficiency was dependent on circulatory factors. Following Mosso's work, many experiments have been conducted to show certain cardiovascular factors to be related to "good" physical condition.

It has been found that the functional organic condition of the body, insofar as it is related to the strength and endurance of the heart and the efficiency of the circulatory-respiratory systems, is reflected in the ability to sustain stressful activity involving total body action in such activities as running, skiing, swimming, and playing tennis, field hockey, or basketball.

Apart from the development of muscular endurance, the most important physiological adaptation for sustained vigorous activity is the ability of the heart to supply more oxygen than normal to the tissues of the body. This is accomplished by increasing the *cardiac output*—that is, the volume of blood pumped by the heart per minute. The cardiac output depends on (1) the *amount* of blood that is available to be pumped out and (2) the *rate* at which it is being pumped. The amount of blood that is pumped out per beat is referred to as the *stroke volume*, and the rate is determined by the heart's contraction per unit of time.

With the onset of exercise, cardiac output is altered by an immediate increase in both heart rate and stroke volume. The increase in stroke volume is made possible by nearly complete emptying of the left ventricle of the heart (recall the discussion in Chapter 2). The limit of the stroke volume is reached when complete emptying of the ventricle occurs at each beat. Thereafter, further increase in cardiac output depends entirely on an increase in the heart rate.

The available research evidence indicates that during exercise, the heart of the trained person (a person in "good" physiological condition) increases in stroke volume more readily than that of an untrained or a sedentary person. Since the heart of a sedentary individual contains less residual blood at the end of a cardiac contraction than does the heart of the trained person, the point of complete emptying will be reached at a lower level of exercise than in the case of the trained person, and thus a greater increase in heart rate will be required to achieve the same cardiac output. For this reason, the performance of the same level of exercise is usually associated with a greater increase in heart rate in the sedentary person than in the trained person.

The heart rate, therefore, can be used to evaluate the stress imposed by muscular activity upon the heart and the circulation. As a single factor, the heart rate quite accurately depicts the cardiovascular adjustment of the individual to muscular activity.

During recovery after light work, the cardiovascular functions soon return to the pre-exercise resting level. The heavier the load, the higher will be the maximum heart rate and the longer it will take to return to the resting level. The time required for this return to normal is dependent on the condition of the person. The better one's physical condition, the less time is required for return of the pulse rate to normal.

The level of physiological fitness of an individual is probably the most important factor determining the cardiovascular reactions to exercise. Because the oxygen requirements of the body tissues increase in proportion to the intensity of physical exertion, fitness for hard muscular work depends to a great extent on circulation. A very fit individual, as compared with a less fit individual, is able to maintain a slower heart rate during activity, can supply a greater volume of blood with each contraction of the heart, and will recover more quickly after exercise.

Studies of the relationship between age and cardiovascular functions have clearly established that it is physiological condition, and not chronological age, that determines an individual's capacity for exercise. And there is considerable evidence that lack of adequate physical activity is a causative factor in the development of chronic degenerative diseases of the heart and circulatory system.

Procedures for Developing Cardiovascular-Respiratory Endurance

In Rome, in 1960, the American College of Sports Medicine, in cooperation with Italian scientists, conducted a World Forum on Physical Education. Out of this group and with the help of the Japanese, there was formed the International Congress of Sport Sciences which met for the first time at the 1964 Olympic Games in Tokyo. At the 1964 meeting, 268 papers were presented which dealt with the effects of training on the heart and blood vessels. In general, the papers were in agreement that exercise will postpone the onset of changes that aging brings to the heart and blood vessels. One particular paper presented at the Tokyo meeting, reporting on the greater efficiency of the trained heart, presented an exercise program entitled "three tablets of preventive cardiology." This consisted of a daily program of three one-minute exercise periods, strenuous enough to raise the heart rate sixty beats above the resting level with one minute of rest between the exercise periods.*

Examples of activities which are of sufficient intensity to meet the requirements specified in this particular training regimen are running, jumping rope, or stepping up and down on a bench that is approximately 18 inches in height.

Whatever training program is used to develop cardiovascular-respiratory endurance, it appears that it is necessary to impose stress on the heart and the circulation. As a result of engaging in regular, vigorous physical activity, the following physiological adaptations enable an individual to increase in the capacity to perform work over a longer period of time before exhaustion:

1. There is a greater mechanical efficiency as measured in terms of lower oxygen consumption for a given amount of work.

2. There is a higher maximum cardiac output with less increase in pulse rate and blood pressure during submaximal exercise.

3. There is a quicker recovery in pulse rate and blood pressure after submaximal exercise.

---

* See Arthur H. Steinhaus, "Report from Tokyo." *The Physical Educator* **22**, 61–64 (1965).

THE NATURE OF FLEXIBILITY

Since movement of the body and body segments can only occur as a result of action at the joints, flexibility is determined by the state or length of the tissues surrounding the joint. While strength of the muscles, tendons, and connective tissue surrounding the joint serve as protection for the body, less than normal flexibility limits movement possibilities. Thus both static alignment of the body (as in standing) and many dynamic movements depend on a certain range of joint motion. The degree of motion is dependent on several anatomical factors:

a) *The structure of the joints.* Shallow joint sockets have a greater possible range of motion than deep joint sockets. Bony processes, at the elbow, for example, limit the amount of motion at the joint.

b) *The degree of stretch or amount of slack in the ligaments.* This depends on the thickness of the ligaments and the tightness of the ligaments around the joint capsule. Ligaments are tough and strong but not very elastic.

c) *Apposition of bulky tissue.* Any unusual amount of fat accumulation around a joint will restrict motion.

d) *Ligamentous action of muscles.* Muscles are the most important factor in maintaining both the stability and mobility of joints. The mobility at the joint, however, is limited if the muscles have, for one reason or another, become shortened (see Chapter 10). Shortening of one group of muscles may be accompanied by weakness in the opposing muscles. The maintenance of maximum stability as well as mobility of the body is determined in large measure by the degree of strength and flexibility of opposing muscle groups.

There is evidence that flexibility is related to several other conditions. An individual may be more flexible at one time of the day than at another and may be more flexible on a warm day than on a cold day. There also appears to be a difference between *static* flexibility (as in standing) and dynamic flexibility—the ability to make rapid changes from position to position. Some individuals may be very flexible in situations which are static in nature, but relatively inflexible in dynamic situations. In addition, some individuals may be very flexible at one joint in the body but very inflexible in others.

In relation to sport, dance, gymnastic, and aquatic activities, flexibility appears to be a highly specific trait. Each movement skill has unique requirements in terms of the range of movement necessary at each joint to produce maximum efficiency. Any randomly selected flexibility exercise may therefore have little value in relation to a specific activity in which you wish to develop skill. Thus it is important to analyze a skill and choose carefully those flexibility exercises which would stretch the specific muscles involved in the activity (see Chapter 9).

Principles Related to Developing Flexibility

Both *slow stretch* and *sudden stretch* have been advocated in the past as methods for increasing joint mobility. Although there is evidence indicating that either method produces about the same amount of increase in flexibility, the slow stretch method appears to present a safer approach in terms of preventing injury to the muscles and connective tissue. The following procedures are based on the principle of slow stretch and are recommended for increasing joint mobility:

a) The limit of joint motion should be approached gradually and then the movement continued with stretching slightly beyond the point of initial discomfort.

b) The weight of the body or of a part of the body, giving in to gravity, often can be used effectively as the force to bring about the slow stretch of muscles and connective tissue.

c) Whenever possible, stretching should be done under the voluntary control of the individual doing the exercise. That is, the amount of stretch and any associated feelings of discomfort are controlled better by the person doing the exercise than by another individual applying force.

Although Chapter 9 is devoted entirely to various kinds of exercises, you may wish also to consult the Appendix, where a minimal general conditioning program is presented.

SUMMARY

1. Conditioning is a process that prepares an individual to engage in movement tasks with physiological efficiency. The term does not refer to the training and practice of the tasks themselves, but rather to the development of specific qualities that are prerequisites for achieving certain levels of proficiency in performance of the task. The discussion in this chapter has been limited to those qualities that are necessary in varying amounts in most movement situations.

2. Strength is defined as the amount of tension that can be exerted in a single maximum contraction, on the one hand, or as the ability of the muscle to contract against submaximal resistance for a long period of time, on the other. It appears that these two concepts of strength represent points on a continuum that extends from a single maximum contraction to a number of submaximal contractions. If the development of strength limits is desired, then conditioning methods should consist of a few contractions

against maximum resistance. If muscular endurance is desired, then conditioning procedures should consist of a greater number of repetitions against a submaximal resistance. Whatever procedure is employed, the overload principle seems to be the dominating factor in strength development.

3. Cardiovascular-respiratory endurance refers to the capacity of the heart to supply oxygen to the tissues of the body. In order to develop this physiological quality, it is necessary to impose stress on the heart and the circulation. The increase in cardiac output as a result of the conditioning occurs primarily as a result of an increase in stroke volume. This adaptation enables the heart to maintain a slower rate during exercise for the "trained" individual in comparison to the "untrained" individual, and for the heart to return to the resting level more quickly following exercise.

4. Flexibility is determined by the degree of mobility at the joints of the body. While a certain amount of stability at the joints serves as protection, less than normal flexibility limits movement possibilities. The slow stretch method of increasing flexibility at a joint appears to present a safer approach in terms of possible injury to the surrounding muscle and connective tissue.

5. The levels of strength, cardiovascular-respiratory endurance, and flexibility that are required are specific to each sport, dance, aquatic, gymnastic, or daily-life activity. In order to achieve at least a minimum level of skill in an activity or to continue performing an activity without fatigue, it is desirable to consider the physiological demands of the activity and then to compare one's own level of physiological fitness in relation to those demands.

SUGGESTED READING

BROUHA, LUCIEN, "Training," in *Science and Medicine of Exercise and Sports*, edited by Warren R. Johnson. New York: Harper & Row, 1960 (Chapter 21)

CHAPMAN, CARLETON B., AND JERE H. MITCHELL, "The physiology of exercise," *Scientific American* **212**, 88–96 (1965)

DAVIS, ELWOOD CRAIG, GENE A. LOGAN, AND WAYNE C. McKINNEY, *Biophysical Values of Muscular Activity*. Dubuque, Iowa: Wm. C. Brown Company, 1965

KARPOVICH, PETER V., *Physiology of Muscular Activity*. Philadelphia: W. B. Saunders Company, 1966

ROYAL CANADIAN AIR FORCE EXERCISE PLANS FOR PHYSICAL FITNESS. New York: Pocket Books, Inc. (by special arrangement with *This Week Magazine*), (rev.) 1962

STEINHAUS, ARTHUR H., *Toward an Understanding of Health and Physical Education*. Dubuque, Iowa: Wm. C. Brown Company, 1963

part III
PRINCIPLES
IN ACTION

The ensuing chapters
are designed to give
you practical suggestions
for applying the
knowledge and
principles for action
gained from the
preceding chapters.
The experiences and
experiments outlined here are
confined to an application of
principles while moving in
various media and have been
created to illustrate principles
and reinforce concepts rather
than to promote your learning
of specific activities.

chapter 9
ACTION MODELS FOR FUNCTIONAL FITNESS

The human body is an instrument for movement. If you are to develop your own unique movement behavior to a level of proficiency that will satisfy you, it is necessary to keep this instrument "sharp" and ready for use. The body can also be likened to a machine, but unlike a man-made machine, which deteriorates with use, the human machine improves with use and deteriorates from lack of it.

The purpose of this chapter is to provide some materials that will help you make an assessment of your "machine" and suggest ways of improving its functional fitness relative to posture, selected components of physical fitness, and capacity for relaxation.

POSTURE

The word posture quite literally means position. As you go about your daily routine your body assumes hundreds of different positions in order for you to accomplish whatever it is you wish to do. Right now as you are reading this chapter you may be seated in a comfortable chair with the book in your lap and your legs curled under you. You have to walk a great deal each day just to get from one class to another. In the course of any day you stand, sit, walk, run, push, pull, lift, carry, stoop, lean, lie down, get up, climb and descend stairs, and do many other things. What are the fundamental concepts that you should know in order to develop and maintain relatively efficient postural habits in your daily activities?

First of all, you should understand that *good posture is the result of proper body alignment.* We are constantly subject to the downward pull of gravity in every position we may assume. Several muscle groups in the body are called antigravity muscles because it is their responsibility to maintain the body in an upright position against the pull of gravity. Proper body

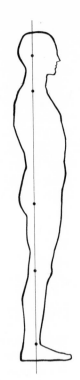

Fig. 9–1. Postural alignment. The centers of gravity of body segments (head, upper trunk, lower trunk, and legs) are aligned with the center of the supporting base (feet).

alignment allows the antigravity muscles to perform their task with the least amount of effort. The laws of equilibrium (Chapter 3) may serve as a partial guide in determining what good alignment in any position should be.

To review briefly, balanced alignment in any position occurs when the centers of gravity of the body segments above the base are directly over the center of the supporting base. The major body segments with which we are concerned in evaluating postural alignment are the head, upper trunk (chest area), lower trunk (pelvis), and lower extremities. For example, in the standing position the head should be balanced directly over the shoulders, the shoulders over the hips, the hips over the long bones of the thighs, and the entire body should be balanced over the base of support—in this case, the feet (see Fig. 9–1). This system of superincumbent segments places the body in a position to resist the downward pull of gravity with the least amount of muscular effort and strain on the ligaments and tendons, which serve (in addition to the bones) as supporting structures. Proper body alignment also presents a more poised and aesthetically pleasing appearance.

A second major concept to remember about posture is that it is *highly individualized*. There can be no single standard for "good posture." There are some general guidelines that may be used for evaluating posture, but because of the many individual differences in body build, weight distribution, and joint mobility, it would be foolish to try to fit everyone into the same postural mold.

The third and probably most important concept to remember is that *posture* (or the positions one assumes repeatedly) *is a habit*. Thus, as with any other habit, it is the product of learning—or more accurately, of *over-learning*. By the time you reach college age your postural habits are quite well established. Your alignment may be essentially correct or faulty, but to you it *feels* "good" or "comfortable." After evaluating your posture you may wish to make some adjustments or corrections. To do this, you will have to replace faulty habits with improved ones by repeated conscious practice of proper body alignment. You must constantly correct and even overcorrect your present alignment habits until old positions no longer feel comfortable. You must learn to develop an awareness or "feel" for what is balanced alignment, and incorporate this new series of sensations into your vocabulary of postural habits.

Evaluation of Standing Alignment

The basic criterion used in the assessment of body alignment is the standing posture. Although standing is only one of many postures assumed in the course of a day, evaluation of it serves as a point of departure for judging many points quickly and accurately. The self-evaluation form given in Worksheet 9–1 is intended to help you make a cursory assessment of your *normal* standing posture. The directions given next will assist you in making accurate observations.

First, provide yourself with the following:

1. A *plumb line*. This can be an ordinary string suspended freely overhead with some kind of small weight attached to the bottom. Do not allow the weight to touch the floor. The suspended string will serve as a visual guide for the line of gravity.

2. A *partner*. For best results you should have someone else observe you, and vice versa. If you try to look at yourself in a mirror you will have to turn your head or otherwise disturb your normal standing posture.

3. A pencil and the evaluation form in Worksheet 9–1.

Side view. Assume your own normal, comfortable standing posture with your side next to the plumb line so that it will bisect your body into two approximately equal halves—front and back. Do not touch the line. Do not try to "stand up straight." You are trying to evaluate your *habitual* standing posture, *not* what you think "good" posture might be. Have your partner look at the following points and make checks in the appropriate spaces on your check sheet.

1. *Body weight:* Sight the overall body balance. The weight should be *centered* evenly over the feet. *Deviations:* Weight shifted forward over the balls of the feet; weight shifted backward over the heels.

2. *Body extension:* When the body is viewed as a whole, it should appear comfortably extended. *Deviation:* Body slumped.

3. *Head:* The head should appear to be evenly balanced over the shoulder. A hypothetical line from the lobe of the ear to the tip of the shoulder should be vertical (unless the shoulders have been shifted forward). Use your plumb line as a guide. *Deviations:* Head tilted forward or back.

4. *Shoulders:* The shoulders should appear to be evenly balanced over the hips. A hypothetical line from the tip of the shoulder to the center of the hip joint should appear vertical (unless either shoulders or hips have been shifted markedly). *Deviations:* Shoulders shifted forward or back.

5. *Chest:* During normal breathing, the chest should appear high but not overly expanded. *Deviation:* Chest depressed.

6. *Upper back:* The upper back in the normal position should appear *slightly rounded.* This slight rounding represents the normal anterior-posterior convex curve in the dorsal (upper) section of the spinal column. *Deviations:* Markedly rounded; flat.

7. *Shoulder blades:* The scapulae or shoulder blades should appear essentially *flat.* You may wish to check the position of the scapulae from the back view also. *Deviation:* Scapulae protruding like "wings."

8. *Lower back:* The lower back (lumbar curve of the spine) should appear *slightly concave.* *Deviations:* Flat or hollow.

9. *Abdomen:* The abdomen should appear *slightly rounded* or *flat.* If the abdominal musculature is in proper condition this slight rounding is due to a deposit of fat that is particularly characteristic of women, and should not be confused with abdominal protrusion due to "sagging" or weakened muscles. *Deviation:* Protruding abdomen.

10. *Knees:* The knees should appear to be slightly flexed or "easy." *Deviations:* Hyperextended ("locked") or bent (flexed too much).

Back view. Stand with your back to the plumb line and center yourself so that the line bisects your body into two symmetrical halves—right and left. The line should appear to follow the line of your spinal column and drop directly between your legs and feet. Again assume your *natural* standing posture, with the feet slightly separated. Have your partner look at the following points and make checks in the appropriate spaces on your check sheet.

1. *Head:* The head should appear centered over your shoulders. *Deviations:* Tilted to the right or left.

2. *Shoulders:* The shoulders should appear level or even. The line of the crest of the shoulders should be perpendicular to the plumb line. *Deviations:* Right shoulder low, or left shoulder low.

3. *Hips:* The hips should appear level or even. An easy way to check this is to look at the spaces between the arms and the body at hip level. The spaces should be nearly the same size and shape. *Deviations:* Right hip high, or left hip high. (Space will appear smaller on the high side.)

Validation of the results of alignment check. You should keep in mind that you are making a *very cursory* assessment of your standing alignment. If you were to make several checks in the same way, the results might not agree with one another. It takes practice to make an evaluation that is essentially accurate. You may wish to repeat the assessment more than once in order to be sure the results accurately reflect your normal standing alignment.

WORKSHEET 9–1   Evaluation of Standing Alignment

Side View	*Normal*	*Deviations*
1. Body weight:	Centered_____	Forward_____ Back_____
2. Body:	Extended_____	Slumped_____
3. Head:	Balanced over shoulders_____	Forward_____ Back_____
4. Shoulders:	Balanced over hips_____	Forward_____ Back_____
5. Chest:	High_____	Depressed_____
6. Upper back:	Slightly rounded_____	Markedly rounded_____ Flat_____
7. Shoulder blades:	Flat_____	Protruding_____
8. Lower back:	Normal curve_____	Flat_____ Hollow_____
9. Abdomen:	Slightly rounded_____ Flat_____	Protruding_____
10. Knees:	Easy_____	Hyperextended_____ Bent_____
Back View		
1. Head:	Centered_____	Right_____ Left_____
2. Shoulders:	Even_____	Low right_____ Low left_____
3. Hips:	Even_____	High right_____ High left_____

Evaluation of Muscle Shortening

Another important area in which you should make a self-assessment is the condition of the muscle groups that are primarily responsible for the maintenance of body alignment. It is not possible to say that shortening in a given muscle group is the cause of a specific postural deviation, but tight muscles do resist postural correction. We provide below a series of flexibility tests for five important muscle groups that have primary responsibility in the maintenance of proper postural alignment. Use Worksheet 9–2 in making your evaluation.

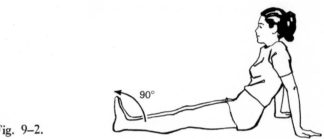

Fig. 9–2.

Test 1. Gastrocnemius and soleus muscles (calf of the leg). Sit down on the floor with your legs extended (see Fig. 9–2). Lean back slightly and rest the weight of your upper body on your hands; keep your arms extended. Attempt to *dorsiflex* your ankles to right angles. Keep your knees extended. If you cannot do this your *gastrocnemius* and *soleus* muscles need some stretching.

Fig. 9–3.

Test 2. Hamstring muscles (back of the thigh). Lie on your back, stretch your arms out at shoulder level, palms of hands facing upward and resting on the floor (see Fig. 9–3). Bend your elbows and rotate at the shoulder joint until your forearms are at right angles to your upper arms, backs of hands and forearms still resting on floor. Lift one leg into the air, keeping the knees of both the resting leg and the lifted leg straight. Keep flexing at the hip until the lifted leg is at a 90° angle with your body. Lower the lifted leg and repeat the lifting action with the other leg. If you cannot place each leg at the 90° angle your *hamstring* muscles may need stretching.

Fig. 9–4.

Test 3. Hip flexors. Lie on your back. Flex one knee and with the arms pull the thigh of that leg to the chest (see Fig. 9–4). Keep your extended leg on the floor with knee *extended*. Do this same movement with other leg. If you cannot do this while keeping the extended leg *straight* and *on the floor* your *hip flexors* may need stretching.

Fig. 9–5.

Test 4. Lumbar extensors (lower back). Take a "long sitting" position, knees extended. Reach for your toes and try to touch them with your fingertips (see Fig. 9–5). If you have difficulty in rounding your lower back when you do this you may need to stretch the muscles called the *lumbar extensors.*

← Resting on floor   Fig. 9–6.

Test 5. Pectoral muscles (chest). Lie on your back and clasp your hands behind your head. Flex your knees *slightly* (see Fig. 9–6). When you are in this position your elbows should rest on the floor without any strain. If you must force your elbows to the floor you probably need to stretch your *pectoral muscles.*

WORKSHEET 9–2   Self-Assessment of Muscle Shortening

Circle the appropriate number for each test.

Key: 1 = you can do the test with ease
2 = you feel some strain
3 = you feel great strain or cannot do it at all

1	2	3	Test 1 (Gastrocnemius and soleus)
1	2	3	Test 2 (Hamstring muscles)
1	2	3	Test 3 (Hip flexors)
1	2	3	Test 4 (Lumbar extensors)
1	2	3	Test 5 (Pectoral muscles)

Muscles that need stretching	Suggested exercises (see pp. 114–116)

With completion of the Standing Alignment Worksheet and the Muscle Testing Worksheet you have made some initial steps in learning about your own postural alignment habits and the condition of important muscle groups that have major responsibilities in the maintenance of good posture. If you have found alignment deviations, your job is to correct them, first by *developing an awareness* for proper alignment in the standing as well as other habitual postures, then by *practicing* the new, more correct alignment until you have established a set of new postural habits. If you have detected muscle shortening in certain groups you can begin to correct this by engaging in certain remedial exercises. Activities that will assist in the development of proper postural alignment are presented on pages 114–116.

EXERCISE ACTION MODELS

Earlier in this chapter we mentioned that the body may be considered a machine and that it improves with use. You may be the kind of person who regularly engages in some kind of strenuous movement activity such as tennis or swimming, which provides enjoyable physical recreation as well as helping you maintain an adequate level of physical fitness. But chances are that as a college student you engage in sedentary activities. You may enjoy physical activity but feel you do not have time for it in your busy schedule. You may *not* enjoy movement activities, but wish to maintain your body in reasonable physical condition for appearance' sake. It is not the purpose of this chapter to deal in detail with the values of fitness, but rather to provide appropriate materials for you to use if you hold physical fitness as a value and wish to improve your level of fitness through the medium of an exercise program. One such program is given in Appendix I. Here, however, we present a more detailed discussion of how a good program can be planned and implemented, and provide a sample program that leaves room for adaptation to your own individual needs.

Before one can know what physical fitness is, or how much of it one should have, one should ask himself the question, "Fit for what?" A general statement that will serve as a guideline is that one should be fit enough to meet one's daily responsibilities without undue fatigue, and still have a reserve for recreation and emergencies. Physical fitness is thus a highly personalized quality; the level of fitness that the office secretary requires is quite different from that required by the concert ballerina. To increase *your* level of fitness you need to analyze the specific needs and demands of your own routine of living.

Furthermore, in order to plan a sensible program of exercises you should know something about the components of physical fitness and plan a program that will increase your level of fitness in each one. As you recall from Chapter 8, these components are:

1) Muscular strength—the amount of tension which can be exerted in a single contraction.

2) Muscular endurance—the ability to continue submaximal contractions over a period of time.

3) Cardiovascular-respiratory endurance—the ability of the heart to supply oxygen to the tissues of the body by increasing the amount of blood pumped by the heart per minute.

4) Flexibility—range of motion possible about the joints.

When planning your exercise program, you should include exercises that will develop muscular strength and endurance in *all major muscle groups*;

exercises that will develop flexibility in those joints that are particularly involved in the maintenance of good posture; and exercises that involve vigorous total body activity (such as running or jumping rope) and thus will increase cardiovascular-respiratory endurance. In addition, you may wish to include exercises to meet limited and specific needs, such as to reduce neuromuscular tension or to "tone up" certain muscle groups to improve your postural alignment.

Whatever your own needs and desires may be with regard to improving or maintaining your level of fitness, there are certain principles which you should observe for developing any or all of the components of physical fitness.

Principles for Developing the Components of Physical Fitness

First let us review some of the material presented in Chapter 8. In order for you to increase muscular strength and/or muscular endurance you must plan exercises that utilize the "overload" principle. Recall that in accord with this principle, one must increase muscular tension over that which was previously exerted. In other words, one must increase the load against which the muscle is exerting force in order that improvement may occur. Recall also that there are two ways in which the overload principle can be applied. During exercise one may gradually increase the resistance against which one is working (for example, lift progressively heavier objects); or one may hold the resistance constant and gradually increase the number of repetitions of the exercise (for example, perform a progressively greater number of sit-ups). The first kind of exercise (increasing the weight or resistance) will develop the quality we have called muscular strength, while the second kind of exercise (increasing the repetitions) will develop the quality called muscular endurance.

In order to increase cardiovascular-respiratory endurance one can again apply the overload principle. Cardiovascular-respiratory endurance is best achieved by engaging in exercises that require total body activity, such as running, climbing stairs or jumping rope. A typical exercise would be stepping up and down on a bench. In this exercise, resistance is minimum (the body weight), repetition or duration is maximum (until you tire), the pace is held constant (submaximum), and the distance is constant (height of step 12–18 inches).

Adequate flexibility or joint mobility is necessary for both static body alignment and dynamic movement situations. Both slow stretching and sudden stretching exercises have been advocated in the past for increasing joint mobility. While either method seems to produce the desired result, exercises that prescribe slow stretching seem to be safer in terms of possible injury to the muscles and connective tissues. Also, slow stretching exercises are less likely to result in muscular soreness during or after the exercise bout.

In selecting flexibility exercises one should adhere to the following principles:

1. The limit of joint motion should be approached gradually and then the movement continued slightly beyond the point of mild discomfort.

2. The weight of a part of the body, giving in to gravity, often can be used effectively to bring about the slow stretch of muscle and connective tissues.

3. Stretching should be done under the *voluntary control of the individual.*

By keeping in mind these basic principles for developing the components of physical fitness, you will be better prepared to make an intelligent selection of exercises for a specific purpose or to design a general exercise program for increasing your overall physical fitness. The remainder of this chapter will present some sample programs that you may wish to adopt unchanged or modify for your own particular purposes.

ACTION MODEL NO. 1: CIRCUIT TRAINING

In recent years an exercise method called circuit training has become increasingly popular as a technique for developing certain components of physical fitness. It is a method of fitness training that aims to increase muscular strength, muscular endurance, and cardiovascular-respiratory endurance. The exercise "circuit" consists of a series of exercises that are carefully arranged and numbered consecutively, each to be performed in its own given area, which is referred to as a station. One may perform the circuit in a gymnasium, but it is just as feasible to design a circuit to be executed in a corridor, recreation room, or dormitory room. The performer moves easily from one exercise station to another doing a prescribed amount of "work" at each station until the circuit is completed. Normally one performs the circuit more than once, usually three times, but there is no magic in this number. The principle of progressive overload is applied by increasing the work load at each station or reducing the time it takes to complete the entire circuit or a combination of both.

Exercises for the circuit are selected on the basis of the specific exercise needs of the performer. The number of repetitions performed at each station as well as the amount of time needed to complete a series of laps around the circuit are determined on the basis of the performer's own present level of fitness. One of the greatest advantages to circuit training as a method of developing fitness is that it can be highly personalized to meet individual needs and desires.

Steps in planning a circuit

1) Preliminary considerations
   a) Define your objectives so that you will have clearly in mind what you hope to gain from participating in the circuit. In other words, ask yourself the question "fit for what?"
   b) Assess your present capabilities carefully. Be sensible about starting at a level which is realistic and safe.

2) Selecting exercises
   a) Exercises included should be strenuous.
   b) Exercises should be simple.
   c) Exercises should be standardized.
   d) Each exercise should contribute to one of your preestablished objectives.
   e) Exercises should reflect a balance, so that all areas of your musculature receive proper attention. For example, you should include exercises for arms and shoulder girdle, abdomen, upper and lower back, and buttocks, thighs, and legs.
   f) Exercises should not require equipment or facilities that you do not readily have available.
   g) The amount of time you are willing to spend each day should be a factor in determining the number as well as the difficulty of the exercises which you select.

3) Constructing the circuit
After exercises are carefully selected, do the following:
   a) Establish the *order* in which the exercises are to be performed. Avoid placing exercises one after another which involve the same muscle groups.
   b) Establish the *placement* of exercise stations in the area in which you intend to work so that you can move easily from one area to the next. The distance between stations will be determined largely by the amount of space within which you must work.

4) Setting the beginning load or "dosage"
In order to determine the appropriate number of repetitions of each exercise as well as the target time for completing the circuit, it is necessary to test yourself over a two-day period. This is called the test-retest system and should be used initially as well as every time you wish to increase the dosage because you have met one set of goals.

   To establish the number of repetitions you should do at each exercise station, on the first day do the following:
   a) Execute one lap of the circuit by doing each exercise the *maximum* number of times. Do the exercises *in the order* they are to be performed at each station. Record the number done on each exercise.

In the case of exercises which you could do indefinitely (such as toe touching) do them for a specified period of time (usually 30 seconds or 1 minute is sufficient).

b) Take a rest period between each exercise—one or one and a half minutes. Keep the rest period constant throughout the circuit.

c) Reduce the number of repetitions on each exercise by $\frac{1}{2}$ for a three-lap circuit (or by $\frac{2}{3}$ for a two-lap circuit). This figure for each station represents the initial "dosage." For example, if you could do 16 sit-ups the first day, your sit-up dosage for the first level of the circuit would be 8. If isometric exercises are included they will not require any change in number of repetitions.

5) On the second day you will establish the "target time" or the amount of time that will be your goal for running three laps of the circuit.

a) Perform three consecutive laps of the circuit, using the dosage you established the day before. Note your starting time.

b) Do not rest between stations.

c) Note the time it takes you to complete the three laps.

d) Reduce this time by $\frac{1}{4}$ or $\frac{1}{3}$; this figure will represent your target time for three consecutive laps for the first level of your training program.

After you have constructed the circuit and established the dosage, you should execute the circuit once each day until you have reached your target time for the completion of the three laps. Then you can set new goals for yourself for further improvement by repeating the test-retest system, establishing new load doses at each station and keeping the target time constant or reducing the target time and keeping the initial load doses constant or a combination of the two. Your decision as to how to increase the demands of the circuit will depend on the amount of time you have to spend and the level of fitness you wish to achieve. If you get to the stage where improvement is very difficult, you may wish to hold both target time and load dosage constant, thus engaging in a "maintenance" regimen.

Two final hints which will help you get the most out of your circuit: first, be sure to *execute each exercise properly*; and second, *keep a careful record of your performance and progress*. An example of a record sheet is included in Worksheet 9–3, for use with the circuit described in the following pages or for one you have constructed yourself.

Now you have all the basic information you need to engage in the circuit training method for developing physical fitness. Circuits may be constructed for any specialized purpose as well as for the development of general fitness. You might wish to include exercises which will help you get into condition for the skiing season or the tennis season. The one component of fitness which is not emphasized in circuit training is flexibility. You may wish to engage in some appropriate exercises which will develop this quality in addition to running the circuit.

WORKSHEET 9–3   Sample Circuit Record

Date

Exercise	(1) ____		(2) ____		(3) ____	
	Test Max.	Dose	Test Max.	Dose	Test Max.	Dose
1						
2						
3						
4						
5						
6						
7						
8						
9						
Initial Time						
Target Time						

Performance Record

Date	Time	Date	Time

SAMPLE EXERCISE CIRCUIT

Overall Purpose. To increase the level of general physical fitness.

Exercise 1. Bench or chair stepping

Purpose: To develop cardiovascular-respiratory endurance

Directions: Stand facing a bench or chair that is firmly stabilized. (Height of bench or chair should be 12–18 inches.) Step up with your left foot, then, extending your knee, bring the right foot alongside the left and put your weight on it. Step down with your left foot first; then bring the right one down and place your weight on it. (See Fig. 9–7.) Continue to step up and down for one minute. Be sure your knees are fully extended when both feet are on the bench. Count the number of times (up and down counts as one) that you are able to perform the exercise in one minute. A stopwatch or clock egg-timer is useful for this exercise.

Modification of this exercise to make it more strenuous may be made in two ways: (1) hold the time constant and increase the number of repetitions per minute or, (2) hold the number of repetitions constant and reduce the time.

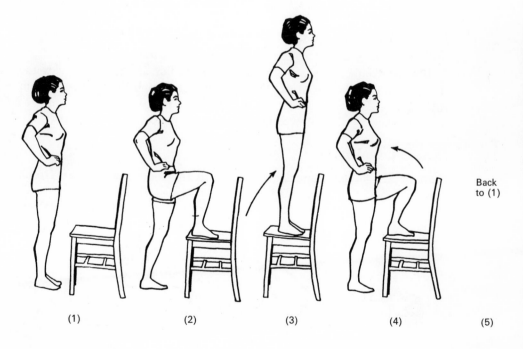

(1)   (2)   (3)   (4)   (5)

Back
to (1)

Fig. 9–7.

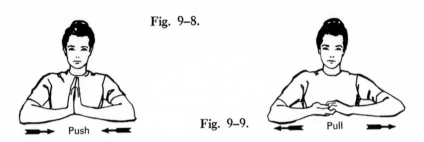

Fig. 9–8.

Fig. 9–9.

Push

Pull

Exercise 2. Isometric push

Purpose: To develop muscular strength of the arm and shoulder girdle adductors.

Directions: Abduct your arms from your body, flex at the elbows, bring palms together. With elbows at shoulder height and pointed away from the body, push the palms together as hard as possible. Then relax. (See Fig. 9–8.)

This exercise will not need modification to increase its difficulty. As strength increases, the maximum contraction against the resistance will automatically become greater.

Exercise 3. Isometric pull

Purpose: To develop muscular strength of the arm and shoulder girdle abductors.

Directions: Abduct your arms from your body, flex at the elbows, flex the fingers, and lock the fingertips. With hands locked, pull the arms away from each other as hard as possible. Then relax. (See Fig. 9–9.)

This exercise will not need modification for increasing its difficulty.

Exercise 4. Curl sit-ups

Purpose: To develop muscular endurance in the abdominal muscles (trunk flexors).

Back to (1)

(1)   (2)   (3)

Fig. 9–10.

Directions: Assume a hook lying position with your knees flexed and your feet flat on the floor. You may need to have your feet stabilized by placing your toes under something heavy or by having a partner hold them down. Clasp your hands behind the back of your head. Point your elbows directly upward with forearms touching the side of your face. Curl your body upward so that the head leaves the floor first, then the shoulders, then the back, etc. Touch your elbows to your knees. Curl back down reversing the order with the head touching the floor last. (See Fig. 9–10.)

Modification of this exercise to make it more strenuous is made by increasing the number of repetitions.

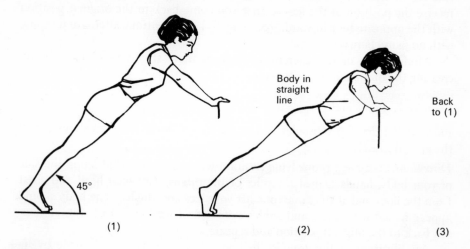

Fig. 9–11.

Exercise 5. Body lowering and raising from an inclined position

Purpose: To develop muscular endurance in the arm and shoulder girdle flexors and extensors.

Directions: Find a stable surface that will support you and that is about waist height, such as the edge of a desk, a dresser, or the back of a chair. Place your hands on the surface, fingers pointing away from you and arms approximately shoulder width apart. While grasping the surface, with elbows extended, take several short steps backward until your body (held straight) makes about a 45° angle with the floor. Lower your chest toward the surface by flexing at the elbows and raise it back to its original position with elbows fully extended. (See Fig. 9–11.) Your body should move up and down as *one unit.* Do not reach with the head. Keep the spine straight and in line with the legs. You may need to have your feet stabilized from behind so that they do not slip backward.

Modification of this exercise to make it more strenuous is made by increasing the number of repetitions.

Exercise 6. Alternate jumps

Purpose: To increase leg power (hip, knee, and ankle extensors) and cardiovascular-respiratory endurance.

Directions: Assume a forward-stride stand with your feet approximately 15–18 inches apart. Lower your trunk until the ankle, knee, and hip of the forward leg are markedly flexed (thigh and trunk at about right angles to one another; rear leg extended with ball of foot touching floor). Jump into the air and reverse the position of the legs so that you come back to the original position with the opposite foot forward. (See Fig. 9–12.) Continue alternate jumping with no pause between jumps.

Modification of this exercise to make it more strenuous is made by increasing the number of repetitions.

Exercise 7. Prone arch

Purpose: To develop muscular endurance in the back and leg extensors and the gluteal muscles.

Directions: Assume a prone-lying position with your arms held along the side of your body, hands against the sides of the thighs. Lift your head and chest from the floor and at the same time lift your legs and thighs. The body should appear arched with knees and ankles extended. (See Fig. 9–13.) Lower yourself back to the original position and repeat.

Modification of this exercise to make it more strenuous is made by increasing the number of repetitions.

Exercise 8. Leg raise

Purpose: To develop muscular endurance in the abductors of the legs.

Directions: Assume a side-lying position with bottom arm extended past your head on a line with your body, so that your head rests on that shoulder. Place the top arm in front of you, palm of the hand on the floor to assist you in maintaining your balance in the side-lying position. Abduct the top leg at the hip joint as far as you can *without causing hip flexion.* Lower the leg until it rests on the bottom one. (See Fig. 9–14.) Continue raising and lowering the top leg until you have performed the specified number of repetitions (up and down counts as one). Roll over on the opposite side and repeat with the other leg. The exercise should be performed at a moderate tempo.

Modification of this exercise to make it more strenuous is made by increasing the number of repetitions.

Fig. 9–12.

(1)   (2)   (3)

Fig. 9–13.

(1)   (2)   (3)

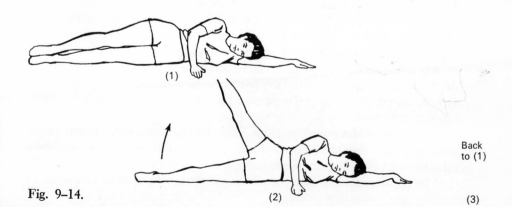

Fig. 9–14.

(1)   (2)   (3)

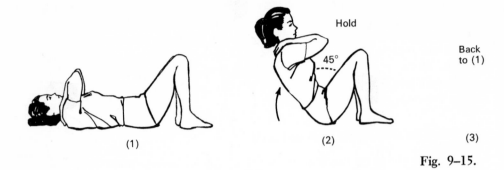

Fig. 9–15.

Exercise 9. Hold-sit

Purpose: To develop muscular strength in the abdominal muscles (trunk flexors).

Directions: Lie on your back and flex your legs at the knees, placing your feet flat on the floor and about six inches from your buttocks. Place your hands on your shoulders. Holding the spine straight, pull the trunk to approximately a 45° angle with the thighs and hold for a long count of ten. (See Fig. 9–15.)

This exercise will *not* need modification in succeeding circuits in order to be more strenuous.

ACTION MODEL NO. 2:
EXERCISES FOR PROMOTING RELAXATION

The modern college student lives a life full of pressure, anxiety, and worry that can cause excess tension. Tension is a term that describes a general condition of activity throughout the body. A certain amount of tension is necessary for action and productivity, but excess tension is a hindrance to successful living. You probably have experienced some of the signs of neuromuscular hypertension at one time or another. For example: Have you experienced periods when you were unable to concentrate on your studies? had trouble sleeping? had frequent headaches? felt some pain in the back of your neck and shoulders? How can you cope with this "tense" feeling, which can interfere with your work?

Exercise provides *one* method for combating neuromuscular hypertension. Mental activity should be balanced with physical activity, for vigorous physical activity diverts you from mental fatigue and produces in its place a healthy state of physical fatigue. But you may not always have time to engage in vigorous physical activity in order to reduce "nervous tension"—you may *have* to study for eight straight hours without much of a "break." In such a situation, the series of exercises given here will assist you in relieving tension in certain muscle groups that are most likely to be affected. They do not require special equipment nor a great deal of space, and do not require you to spend a lot of your precious time. They can be helpful in preventing muscular tenseness as well as relieving it.

Exercises for relaxing the head and neck

1. Sit comfortably on the floor. Lean back on your hands. Allow your head to *drop* forward. Try not to *pull* the head down. You should feel the muscles at the back of your neck being stretched by the weight of your head. Repeat, allowing the head to drop backward, then to the left and right.

2. Head swaying: while sitting comfortably, allow the head to drop forward as above. Now roll the head to one side until your ear is directly over your shoulder. Then let your head swing forward and downward and over to the other side. Continue until you can feel that the muscles at the back and sides of the neck are being stretched and beginning to relax.

Exercises for relaxing the shoulder girdle

1. While sitting on a chair or standing, hold your spine erect and lift one shoulder at a time, then allow it to *drop* back into place. Keep your arms relaxed and hanging at the sides. Try both shoulders at the same time. You should feel a strong muscle contraction as you elevate the shoulder; then you should feel a stretching or passive lengthening in the muscles as you allow gravity to cause the shoulders to *drop*.

2. While seated comfortably on a chair with your arms hanging at your sides, contract your back muscles so that you are pulling the shoulder blades toward one another. Now relax and let them return or "fall back" to their original position.

Exercises for relaxing the arms

1. Select a soft surface such as a rug, mat, or bed. Lie down on your back with arms resting at sides. Lift one arm about six inches in the air. Hold it there briefly, then allow it to *fall* back to your side. Now repeat with the other arm. You should feel the arm *drop* to your side.

2. Lie down on your stomach on a bed or table so that you can allow one arm to "dangle" *freely* over the edge. Lift the arm forward and upward toward your head; then relax and allow it to swing freely like a pendulum

until motion ceases. You should *not* use any muscular effort for the swing. Repeat with the opposite arm.

3. While sitting in a chair, allow your arms to hang freely from your sides. Shake your arms vigorously; then relax them. Repeat several times.

Exercises for relaxing the trunk

1. Stand in a side-stride position. Gradually allow your head to drop forward toward your chest, then curl your spine so that the trunk drops forward as far as possible. Allow your arms to hang freely. You should feel as though you are giving in to gravity with your relaxed spine hanging from your pelvis. Now slowly lift your trunk back to an erect position, starting with the lower back and lifting the head last.

2. Assume the forward-stride hanging position described above. Now toss your entire trunk loosely from side to side about your legs. Try to initiate the movement from the lower back. Allow the arms to swing freely.

Exercises to relax the legs

1. In a standing position, place your weight on one leg and shake the opposite one vigorously. Try to keep the ankle and foot passive. Repeat with the other leg.

2. In a back-lying position, with legs slightly separated, stretch or extend both legs and ankles strongly. Then relax suddenly. Keep your upper body, head, and arms relaxed.

ACTION MODEL NO. 3:
EXERCISES FOR STRENGTHENING POSTURAL MUSCLES

Postural alignment was discussed at some length at the beginning of this chapter. In the following pages are several exercises that would be helpful for "toning up" certain key groups of antigravity muscles.

Exercises for control of pelvic tilt

Pelvic tilt represents increased curvature of the lumbar spine and lack of abdominal control.

1. Stretch exercises

    a) Assume a back-lying position on the floor with arms extended at the sides. Press your lower back (lumbar spine) to the floor. (Contraction of the gluteals will assist you in flattening your lumbar spine.) Stretch or extend your legs and feet; arms stretched above the head. While stretching your body, the lumbar area should maintain contact with the floor.

The following exercises are a variation of the stretch exercise just described.

b) When performing this exercise and the next one it is important that your *lumbar spine is in contact with the floor*. Stretch the arm and leg on your right side while relaxing the arm and leg on your left side.

c) Stretch your right arm and left leg diagonally across your body while relaxing the left arm and the right leg. Reverse: stretch your left arm and right leg while relaxing your right arm and left leg.

2. Sit-up progressions. The following exercises are a suggested progression for sit-ups which will allow for sequential action of your spine and help to strengthen the abdominal muscles.

Assume a back-lying position, knees slightly flexed, and arms extended at the sides. *Your lumbar spine is to maintain contact with the floor during each of the exercises,* except in (d).

a) Lift your head and shoulders off the floor. Relax.

b) Lift your head and shoulders off the floor slightly more than in position (a). Relax.

c) Lift your head and shoulders off the floor slightly more than in position (b). Relax.

d) Lift your head and shoulders off the floor and assume a sitting position.

After successful performance of controlled sit-ups, try the following progression:

a) With your chest leading, lift your head and shoulders from the floor. (Head is dropped back in a relaxed position.) Relax.

b) With your chest leading, lift your head and shoulders from the floor slightly more than in position (a). Relax.

c) With your chest leading, lift your head and shoulders from the floor slightly more than in position (b). Relax.

d) With your chest leading, assume a sitting position. From this sitting position, gradually curl down to a back-lying position. Allow your head to be the last segment of your body to come into contact with the floor.

Exercises for alignment of upper trunk and head

1. Assume a back-lying position with knees flexed, feet flat on the floor. Stretch the top of your head upward and flatten your neck onto the floor. At the same time pull your shoulder blades down and backward (towards one another).

2. Assume a sitting position with knees flexed and hands clasped around knees. Relax your spine and allow your head to drop toward your knees. Starting with the lower back, straighten your spine vertebra by vertebra, allowing the head to rise last. Relax and repeat several times.

Exercises for shoulder girdle alignment

1. Assume a prone-lying position with forehead resting on the floor. Clasp your hands behind your back. Pull your shoulder blades (adduct them) together strongly, then relax. To make this exercise more taxing, after the shoulder blades are adducted, unclasp your hands and lower them slowly to your sides. Release the shoulder blade adduction last.

2. Assume a crossed-leg sitting position (tailor sit). Raise the arms sideward (adduct them) to shoulder level with elbows flexed at right angles and forearms horizontal, palms facing one another. Now, simultaneously rotate your forearms upward, so your fingers point directly toward the ceiling, and pull your shoulder blades together (adduct them). Then lower your arms to your sides while maintaining the shoulder blade adduction. Relax.

Two worksheets, Appendixes II and III, can be used for keeping a record of your improvement.

SUGGESTED READING

JACOBSON, EDMUND, *You Must Relax*. New York: McGraw-Hill Book Company, Inc., 1957 (Chapter 14)

JOHNSON, PERRY B. *et al.*, *Physical Education: A Problem-Solving Approach to Health and Fitness*. New York: Holt, Rinehart and Winston, 1966 (Chapters 23, 24, 25, 26)

SORANI, ROBERT, *Circuit Training*. Dubuque, Iowa: Wm. C. Brown Co., 1966

WELLS, KATHARINE F., *Posture Exercise Handbook*. New York: The Ronald Press Company, 1963

WILLIAMS, MARION, AND CATHERINE WORTHINGHAM, *Therapeutic Exercise*. Philadelphia: W. B. Saunders Company, 1957

chapter 10
MOVEMENT IN THE
AQUATIC MEDIUM

Man's adaptation to bipedalism as a consistent form of locomotion during the course of evolution has facilitated his movement on land, but has made him less well adapted to propulsion in water. For quadrupeds, the task of adapting to movement in the aquatic medium is relatively easy, since the natural locomotor movements of the organism are employed in both media. Man, on the other hand, has had to devise effective means for traveling under, on, and over water in order to more fully explore his environment.

In our culture today, participation in swimming and other aquatic activities enjoys widespread acceptance. The opportunities for participation are quite abundant: state and national governments are preserving areas with the establishment of parks near rivers, lakes, and seacoasts; cities and towns are building municipal pools; schools and colleges offer a variety of swim and aquatic programs; many other agencies, both private and public, are providing additional facilities and instruction; and more homeowners are installing their own "backyard" pools.

The values each of you hopes to attain from participation in activities in the aquatic medium are apt to be varied, and your purposes for participation will have some effect on the level of proficiency you strive to attain. For some of you, learning only basic essentials is all that may be desired, since the aim is only to participate *safely* in recreational activities such as boating, water skiing, and surfing. Some may enjoy testing themselves through competition. While racing is more popular with younger girls, many college women enjoy the competitive aspects of synchronized swimming. In addition to the competitive aspects, you may also enjoy this activity, either as participant or observer, for its aesthetic qualities, but these qualities are by no means limited to synchronized swimming. Students at all levels of ability, even beginners, can gain appreciation from watching skilled performers and can also experience pleasure from their own performance. A novice may be able to gain as much pleasure from pushing off and gliding smoothly over the surface of the water, even if only for a short distance, as her friend, who can "knife" cleanly through the water lap after lap, using a variety of strokes. Yet again, some of you may wish to utilize your ability to move in the aquatic medium in order to maintain or increase your present level of physical fitness. And finally, some of you will wish to participate just for the fun of it or for the additional social opportunities that are available because you can move at least somewhat effectively in the water.

LEARNING FACTORS

You have examined the many affectors and effectors of human movement in preceding chapters. It is the purpose of this chapter to explore some of these as they particularly apply to learning to move in the aquatic medium. It is assumed that you have a preparatory set and are motivated, perhaps for one or more of the purposes stated above, to learn new skills and improve your present capabilities in this medium.

As was pointed out in Chapter 7, all learning is more effective if it is goal-oriented. Measuring the amount of time it takes to move from one point to another can give you an indication of the effectiveness of a stroke; reducing the time is therefore a valid goal even though your ultimate objective may not be to become a competitive racer. Being able to swim increasingly longer distances without undue discomfort may be another goal. As skill is acquired, both the speed and endurance goals can be made progressively more difficult. The outcomes of your performance in relation to these goals are easily observed, and the objectives may be accomplished through a variety of strokes and skills. You will find, of course, that some skills do not have outcomes that are as easily defined. Knowledge of results of the performance may then depend on both your own and your instructor's subjective perceptual judgments. The learning of stunts or composing of a routine in synchronized swimming are examples of such skills.

Perceptual factors. Recall that to make a practice situation most effective, it is important to attend to concurrent sensory feedback. When moving in the aquatic medium, you will experience sensory cues that are not present in other movement situations. Locomotion on land is usually in an upright or nearly upright position, and the receptors of the inner ear help you to perceive this as a "normal" position. When deviations from this position occur, sensory feedback from these receptors alerts the body for compensating action.

In the aquatic medium, the majority of locomotor movements are executed in a horizontal position and stimuli must now be interpreted in light of this different basic body position. The necessary adjustment is made somewhat easier by the fact that the effect of the force of gravity is lessened in the water. This point will be enlarged upon a little further on in this chapter.

As in other learning situations, visual cues are an important aid to performance, for they help you to remain aware of where you are located in the water. It is difficult for some students to keep their eyes open when the face is in the water. This problem should be overcome as quickly as possible if benefit is to be gained from all sensory modalities. One caution: you should avoid relying too heavily on visual stimuli while swimming. When attempting to propel yourself in a straight path, you may make the mistake of compensating for one mechanical inaccuracy by another if you rely mainly on visual cues for direction. For example, if one arm is pulling more forcefully than the other, which might cause the body to move off course, compensating actions might include kicking harder with the leg on the opposite side of the body or changing the head position. You may be quite unaware of this adjustment, which interferes with maximum stroke efficiency, if you are concentrating too much on visually lining yourself up with a point of reference in the pool.

Concurrent sensory feedback may also be gained through auditory cues. It may be necessary to attend to verbal cues or to a rhythm (when swimming to music). This is not always easy to do, for the sound may be distorted by the water and/or a bathing cap covering the ears. You should also attend to the presence or absence of sounds from your own movements. When you are executing a smooth, gliding type of stroke, for example, there should be almost an absence of auditory stimulation. Therefore, if you hear a splash each time the kick is executed in the breast stroke, there is immediate feedback that the movement is incorrect. Your instructor will assist you in determining which auditory cues should be present or which should be absent for each skill to be learned.

As you have discovered from learning skills in other media, attending to proprioceptive cues may aid in making the practice situation more effective. Changes in joint position are one example. Additional cues can be gained from the various receptors located in the skin (cutaneous receptors). Changes in temperature may indicate to you when body segments are out of the water. The sensations perceived from currents and eddies moving about the body may also provide information concerning performance. Still other cues can be gained from perceiving the presence or absence of resistance to movements of body segments through the water. The absence of resistance to leg movements may indicate to you that the feet are rising too far out of the water in the flutter kick.

Although some stimuli will be employed to a greater extent at different times in the learning process, it is important at all times to utilize sensory input from as many sources as possible.

MECHANICAL FACTORS

Understanding the mechanical concepts that govern efficient movement in the aquatic medium can aid you in determining the relevant perceptual cues and in setting performance goals. Before examining the elements that contribute to efficient performance, it is necessary to explore the differences between moving in this medium and other media. Consideration must be given to (a) contrasts in surfaces against which force is exerted to produce locomotion, (b) the basic body position and base of support utilized, and (c) the relative density of the two media (air and water), and the effects of gravity and buoyancy.

Differences in resistance. In previous discussion you have been shown that in locomotor actions on land, movements are executed that result in the exertion of force through the feet against a resistive surface such as the ground or floor. With every such action there is an equal and opposite reaction; this is why the force is effective in moving you in a direction opposite to its application. The aquatic medium, however, presents some unique mechanical problems. Water, because it is not as resistive as the ground or floor, allows some of the applied force to be dissipated in the direction toward which it is applied. This means that the applied force is not as effective in producing movement in the desired direction.

Differences in support. In the majority of locomotor movements occurring in sports, dance, and everyday activities, the body moves in an upright position with the feet acting as the base of support and the legs supplying the primary moving force. In water, however, most locomotion occurs in a horizontal position, so that (1) your *total body* is the base of support and (2) your legs *and* arms act to produce movement. By contrast to movement on land, the utilization of arms and legs for moving in the water becomes both possible and necessary: possible, because the body is supported in the medium against which it applies force, and necessary, because a good deal of propelling force is dissipated and the density of the water acts as a restrictive factor that moderates progress; thus the body is required to expend additional effort in order to effect movement. Under normal conditions, however, movement of the body or its segments through water is not a total mechanical disadvantage, because the medium aids in supporting the body. Gravitational pull is an ever-present factor in moving on land or in the air, but in water its effect is minimized by buoyancy, which exerts a counteractive upward force on the body.

BUOYANCY

In a discussion of buoyancy an understanding of several principles should be gained so that they may be applied to produce efficient movement skills. For a body to be supported by water its specific gravity must be less than that of water. Specific gravity is the ratio of body weight per unit volume to the weight of an equal amount of water. A body will sink when its specific gravity is greater than that of water, it will be suspended in the fluid when the specific gravity of each is the same, and it will "float" with some part above the surface when its specific gravity is less than that of water. Differences in specific gravity account, to some extent, for the fact that some people "float like corks" and others "sink like rocks."

Body composition is a primary factor affecting a person's ability to be buoyant. The less dense the body is in relation to its weight, the more buoyant it will be. In addition, there is a difference in the specific gravity of different parts of the body. Bones and muscles, because they are more dense, have a higher specific gravity than adipose tissue. In general, the male is larger-boned and more heavily muscled than the female and does not have as much fatty tissue; therefore, men do not float as easily as women. The chest cavity, containing the lungs (which weigh less per unit volume than any other body part), is the most buoyant part of the body, particularly when the lungs are inflated with air.

The center of buoyancy and the center of gravity. Rotary motion outside the aquatic medium is a result of the body's rotation around its center of gravity, but in water rotation occurs around the body's center of buoyancy. As was stated in Chapter 3, the center of buoyancy is simply the center of gravity of the displaced volume of water. In the human body, this point is generally higher than the center of gravity; it is usually located at about chest level, whereas the center of gravity (in an adult female) is usually at hip level. Recall from Chapter 3 that the closer these two points are to each other, the more buoyant the body will be. In most individuals the two points are separated somewhat, and therefore rotation occurs about the center of buoyancy (the feet sink) until the center of gravity falls on a vertical line below the center of buoyancy. Only then can the body float motionlessly.

The amount of rotation that occurs depends on the individual's center of gravity. Therefore, to perform a motionless back-float, an individual with a relatively low center of gravity and high center of buoyancy must modify her body position—she must redistribute her weight and thus raise her center of gravity to a point where it more nearly coincides with her center of buoyancy. This can be accomplished by flexing the knees, which results in the shortening of the longer, heavier levers of the lower extremities. Keeping the arms in the water, extending them forward (or backward, for back-float) past the head, and inflating the lungs may also contribute to making an individual more buoyant.

Conversely, certain adjustments in position may tend to make an individual less buoyant. For example, when body segments are raised above the surface, the weight that is not supported by the water is increased and the surface area of the base of support is decreased. The surface area acting as a support is also reduced when the body assumes a vertical position.

When the body is propelled in a horizontal position, the more buoyant an individual is, the less force will be required to keep the body close to the surface. The expended effort can then be utilized for motion in the desired line of direction. Therefore, by applying your understanding of the principles of buoyancy, and by making intelligent and effective adjustments accordingly, you can increase your success and enjoyment of moving in the aquatic medium.

MOVING EFFICIENTLY IN WATER

Because of the supportive yet nonresistive qualities of water, the horizontal position has been found to be the most efficient for moving through this medium. Numerous strokes have been devised to produce locomotion in water; the stroke you select is dependent on the task to be accomplished.

During the force production phase of any swimming stroke, the arms engage in either a pushing or pulling type of movement, and the legs in a thrusting or squeezing type of action. Recall that, in general, movement in a desired direction occurs when force is applied in the *opposite* direction. Swimming movements must be executed in such a manner that the water becomes as resistive as possible when force is applied against it. Three factors contribute to the most efficient use of energy expended: (1) movements through as wide a range of motion as possible, (2) directing the force so that it is applied as nearly as possible in the direction opposite to the direction in which you wish to go, and (3) keeping the surface area of the part applying the force as great as possible.

Because of the structure of the human body it is not always possible to execute movements which contribute to total efficiency; therefore, the problem becomes one of selecting movements that best accomplish the task at hand. One of two categories of strokes might be employed: strokes with a continuous action, or those which utilize a glide phase. During a stroke which is continuous in nature there is always one part of the body producing force. This type of stroke is employed when *speed* is the major outcome that is desired. For locomotion over longer distances, when *endurance* is the factor, the performer may find that it is more advantageous to utilize a stroke with a glide.

A glide is a period of rest during which no action occurs because the momentum from the previous force production phase is utilized. Since it is more efficient, from the standpoint of energy expenditure, to move at a constant speed, a glide should not continue beyond the point where momentum begins to diminish. If forward momentum ceases, inertia must be overcome when executing the next stroke, and this, of course, requires greater energy expenditure.

Locomotion in the aquatic medium demands that consideration be given to the forces that impede progress. If these are partially or totally overcome, the propulsion phase of execution will be more efficient. Some reduction of resistance may be achieved by applying the principles of propulsion in reverse. For example, at the completion of the force production phase of any stroke there is a problem of placing the limbs in position to repeat the propulsive movement. There is no way to do this without moving some body parts in the opposite direction from that which contributes to force production. The problem, then, is to *minimize* the resistance to the force involved. A partial solution is to perform the recovery movement slowly and to reduce the cross-sectional area. This is facilitated by keeping the arms close to the body during recovery and by maintaining a horizontal position. In some cases it is possible to employ an overwater recovery stroke; this helps reduce resistance to movement, since air is less dense than water. Although the raising of an arm out of water tends to make the body less buoyant, the advantage of the overwater recovery outweighs this disadvantage.

In addition to the water and air resistance encountered in the recovery phase, the swimmer may encounter resistance from skin friction, wave-making effects that come with increased speed, and currents and eddies resulting from the movement of the body during the force production phase.

Stronger resistance than normal is encountered when one is swimming underwater. Because none of the body is above the surface, the cross-sectional area is increased. Furthermore, for the more buoyant individual, increased force must be exerted to keep the body underwater while maintaining motion in the desired direction.

Changing position. Changing position from the horizontal to vertical can most easily be accomplished by flexing the trunk into a tucked position. This reduces the length of body levers and the surface area, and the body can rotate more quickly about its center of buoyancy. Applying arm pressure in the direction opposite to that of the rotation also facilitates change in position. The same principles are operant whether a novice swimmer applies them in order to change quickly from the horizontal position to a standing position in the shallow area of the pool, or a speed swimmer applies them in executing a "tumble turn" at the end of the lap to cut down on the time used for changing direction.

SUMMARY

1. Aquatic activities enjoy widespread cultural acceptance, and opportunities for participation are abundant.

2. The values that each individual hopes to achieve as outcomes from participating in aquatic activities are varied. Among these are: (a) knowledge of basic safety skills, (b) satisfaction from competitive situations, (c) aesthetic pleasure, (d) conditioning values, (e) social opportunities, and (f) fun and enjoyment.

3. Speed and endurance are outcomes of performance that can be measured and utilized in progressive goal-setting.

4. In the aquatic medium there are sensory cues that are not present when moving in other media: changes in skin temperature become more noticeable, sensations are perceived from the flow of currents and eddies about the body, and information is gained from the presence or absence of resistance to movements. The interpretation of all cues is somewhat different, also, for the body must adjust to propulsion in the horizontal position.

5. Attendance to concurrent sensory feedback from visual and auditory stimuli is important, but excessive reliance on vision hinders performance, and verbal auditory or rhythmic auditory cues may be somewhat distorted. The presence or absence of sounds made during movement provides helpful information about performance.

6. Since water is not as resistive as the ground or a floor, propulsion in water presents unique mechanical problems.

7. The total body, in a horizontal position, acts as the base of support during most movement in the aquatic medium. The effect of gravitational pull is minimized by the counteractive upward force of buoyancy.

8. For a body to be supported by water its specific gravity must be less than that of water. Specific gravity is the ratio of body weight per unit volume to the weight of an equal amount of water. Body composition affects a person's ability to be buoyant—bone and muscle are denser and weigh more than adipose tissue.

9. The sinking of the feet results from the body's rotation around the center of the weight of displaced water, i.e., the center of buoyancy. The most buoyant position for the body is one in which the center of buoyancy and the center of gravity are in close proximity.

10. Propulsion is accomplished by the arms, in a pushing or pulling type of movement, and the legs, in a thrusting or squeezing type of action. Movement in a desired direction occurs when force is applied in the opposite direction.

11. It is desirable, during force production, to make movements over as wide a range as possible, to apply the force as nearly in the opposite direction to the intended motion as possible, and to keep the surface area applying the force as broad as possible.

12. Strokes that are continuous in nature are employed when speed is the major outcome desired, and strokes that have a glide phase are utilized when endurance is a factor.

13. During recovery actions it is necessary to minimize resistance by performing movements slowly, reducing cross-sectional area, and/or employing an overwater recovery of the arms.

14. Changing position from the horizontal to vertical is facilitated by flexing the trunk and applying arm pressure in the direction opposite to that of the rotation.

SUGGESTED READING

ARMBRUSTER, D. A., AND LAURENCE E. MOREHOUSE, *Swimming and Diving*. St. Louis: The C. V. Mosby Company, 1950

BROER, MARION, *Efficiency of Human Movement*, Second Edition. Philadelphia: W. B. Saunders Company, 1966 (Chapter 11, pp. 308–323)

BROWN, RICHARD L., *Teaching Progressions for the Swimming Instructor*. Silver Springs, Maryland: Richard L. Brown, 1953

BUNN, JOHN W., *Scientific Principles of Coaching*. Englewood Cliffs, N.J.: Prentice-Hall, Inc., 1964 (Chapter 11, pp. 175–185)

COOPER, JOHN M., AND RUTH B. GLASSOW, *Kinesiology*. St. Louis: The C. V. Mosby Company, 1963 (Chapter 11, pp. 127–130; Chapter 13, pp. 140–175)

LABORATORY EXPERIMENTS

The experiments below have been grouped into general areas in order to illustrate particular principles. Although in each case you are to focus on the specific aspect, you should be aware of other principles that may be operant in the learning of the task. A more meaningful understanding of the concepts involved will be possible if, in addition to attempting to execute the experiments, you observe others as they participate in the activities.

I. INTRODUCTION TO THE MEDIUM

1. Compare walking on land to walking in water that is at about chest depth.

   a) Why is one more easily executed than the other? _____

   _____

   b) What effect would holding the arms out of water have on forward

   propulsion? Why? _____

   _____

2. Move an arm through the water slowly and then as quickly as possible. Utilize different hand surfaces when executing both movements. Repeat with the eyes closed.

   a) What implications does a comparison of fast and slow movements have

   for propelling the body in this medium? _____

   _____

   b) Was there any difference in perceiving the movements in the two

   situations? If you answer yes, why? _____

   _____

II. UNDERSTANDING THE ROLE OF PERCEPTION

A. Concentration on proprioceptive information without vision

1. Swim a width of the pool, eyes open, attempting to travel in a straight line. Repeat with the eyes closed. Have a partner assist you when your eyes are closed so that you will not bump into the side of the pool. Attempt each situation for at least five trials for each stroke you are able to execute. Record the results on the chart in Worksheet 10–1, using the key given with the chart to describe the path you traveled for each trial.

   a) Was there a consistent direction error? If your answer is yes, what

   might be a possible explanation? _____

   _____

   _____

   b) Did you visually imagine the path to be traveled when your eyes were

   closed? _____

WORKSHEET 10–1   Concentration on Proprioceptive Information Without Vision

Stroke	Trial	Visual Cues Present					Visual Cues Absent				
		1	2	3	4	5	1	2	3	4	5

Key: S = Straight path, L = Path veers to left, R = Path veers to right,
Z = Erratic or zigzag path.

Trial	Decision while surfacing		Decision after surfacing	
	Correct	Incorrect	Correct	Incorrect
1				
2				
3				
4				
5				

Trial	Successful	Unsuccessful	What part of sequence gave you the most difficulty?
1			
2			
3			
4			
5			

2. With your eyes closed, surface dive and swim underwater in a circular pattern for as long a distance as you are able. (a) Decide what direction you will be facing *before* you have completed resurfacing. (b) Decide what direction you are facing *after* resurfacing. Place a check in the appropriate column of Worksheet 10–1 after each trial. What sensory cues influenced your decision in each situation?

a) _____

b) _____

3. In a vertical position, with the eyes closed, gently hang on to the side of the pool facing the wall. Take a breath and place your face in the water, letting the feet rise to the surface. When you think you are in a horizontal position, gently push yourself straight out from the side of the pool. Just at the point when you feel your feet begin to sink, kick back to the side. Have a partner observe your performance and make checkmarks in the appropriate columns of Worksheet 10–1. What cues were you concentrating on

in order to know when the horizontal position had been reached? _____

_____

_____

B. Concentration on Rhythmic Stimuli

Prior to learning a new stroke, watch a skilled performer executing it. Analyze the basic rhythmical organization using words, numbers, or symbols of your own choosing, e.g., pull—kick—glide—, 1—2—3—. Then analyze your own rhythmic pattern while performing the stroke (a) early in the learning process, (b) midway in the learning process, (c) after the stroke has been learned. Record your analysis in the appropriate column of Worksheet 10–2 for each stroke learned. Make any other additional comments, e.g., "slower tempo than skilled performer," and indicate which part of the stroke receives the greatest emphasis, if any. Were there changes occurring in your basic rhythmic organization? If so, how did these influence the learning situation?

_____

_____

_____

_____

WORKSHEET 10–2   Concentration on Rhythmic Stimuli

Stroke	Skilled performer		Early	Your own pattern Midway	Learned

III. UNDERSTANDING THE MECHANICAL FORCES AT WORK

A. Buoyancy

In each experiment, attempt as many trials as necessary in order to answer the questions.

1. Inhale deeply and tuck the body into a tight ball, clasping the arms around the legs. Repeat two more times, once inhaling with a regular breath, and once taking a large inhalation and exhaling while the face is in the water.

   a) What part of the body, if any, is above the surface? _____

   _____

   b) What is the relationship of the center of gravity to the center of buoyancy? _____

   _____

   c) Why is it possible for the body to be supported by water? _____

   _____

   _____

2. Perform a float in a prone position, then one in the supine position. The arms should be in relatively the same position for both.

   a) Does the body appear to be more buoyant in one position than the other? If so, what might be a possible explanation? _____

   _____

   _____

3. Float motionlessly in a supine position. Experiment by making the following adjustments in body position and breathing:

   a) Slowly move the arms from the side of the body out to shoulder level until they are extended over head. Pause at various points in the range of motion.

   b) From a position where the legs are together and extended, allow the knees to flex.

   c) With the head resting in the water, slowly tuck the chin toward the chest. Then slowly tilt the head back.

   d) Hyperextend the spine in the thoracic area.

   e) Breathing adjustments: (i) normal respiration; (ii) deep inhalation and shortened exhalation; (iii) deep inhalation, long forced exhalation.

Which of the above adjustments or positions tend to make the body more buoyant? Why?

a) _____

b) _____

c) _____

d) _____

e) _____

4. While in a horizontal (supine) position slowly make adjustments which will cause the body to rotate toward the vertical. Then return to the horizontal.

a) What part of the body serves as the fulcrum during rotation? _____

_____

b) What name has been given to this point? _____

_____

5. Push off from the bottom of the pool into a horizontal position with enough force to enable the body to glide.

a) Is it easier to maintain a horizontal position while motionless or while

moving? Give the reasoning behind your answer. _____

_____

b) Experiment with different positions of the arms and legs while gliding. What positions, for both prone and supine, allow the body to glide a longer distance with the same amount of applied force? Explain your

answer. _____

_____

6. In a vertical position in deep water, lightly hang on to the side of the pool. Then release your hold, and maintain a motionless vertical position with the head close to the surface. Contrast this position to the horizontal float.

a) Which is easier to maintain? Why? _____

_____

b) What happens to the body in the vertical position when the head is

tilted forward? _____

_____ Tilted back? _____

_____

B. Preliminary force production

1. Quickly move from a horizontal to a vertical position.

   a) In what direction is force applied to accomplish this? ⎯⎯⎯⎯⎯⎯

   ⎯⎯⎯⎯⎯⎯⎯⎯⎯⎯⎯⎯⎯⎯⎯⎯⎯⎯⎯⎯⎯⎯

   b) To facilitate the change what adjustments must be made in body position? Why? ⎯⎯⎯⎯⎯⎯⎯⎯⎯⎯⎯⎯⎯⎯⎯⎯⎯⎯⎯

   ⎯⎯⎯⎯⎯⎯⎯⎯⎯⎯⎯⎯⎯⎯⎯⎯⎯⎯⎯⎯⎯⎯

   ⎯⎯⎯⎯⎯⎯⎯⎯⎯⎯⎯⎯⎯⎯⎯⎯⎯⎯⎯⎯⎯⎯

2. In a vertical position move the body above and below the surface.

   a) What actions are necessary to accomplish this with ease? ⎯⎯⎯⎯⎯

   ⎯⎯⎯⎯⎯⎯⎯⎯⎯⎯⎯⎯⎯⎯⎯⎯⎯⎯⎯⎯⎯⎯

   b) In addition to muscular action, what other factor will facilitate the sinking of the body below the surface? ⎯⎯⎯⎯⎯⎯⎯⎯⎯⎯

   ⎯⎯⎯⎯⎯⎯⎯⎯⎯⎯⎯⎯⎯⎯⎯⎯⎯⎯⎯⎯⎯⎯

C. Movement of the body in a supine position

1. Move across the pool utilizing only the arms which must remain under the surface of the water.

2. Execute an action with the legs that is similar to the arms for producing force to move the body.

3. Simultaneously execute both the arm and leg actions to propel the body.

4. While performing each of the above, experiment with the following:

   Range of joint action during force production phase.
   Direction of force application.
   Body surfaces applying force.
   Methods of placing limbs in a position to re-apply force.
   Trunk and head positions.
   Time sequence: slow and fast movements for each phase; hesitation between recovery and force production phases; length of time interval between end of force production and start of next movement.
   Breathing cycle.

   a) What is the most efficient manner in which to execute the parts and the combined action? ⎯⎯⎯⎯⎯⎯⎯⎯⎯⎯⎯⎯⎯⎯⎯⎯

   ⎯⎯⎯⎯⎯⎯⎯⎯⎯⎯⎯⎯⎯⎯⎯⎯⎯⎯⎯⎯⎯⎯

b) Give the reasons for deciding why certain adjustments experimented with were efficient in contributing to movement of the body. _____

D. Movement of the body in a prone position

1. Propel the body forward using a continuous and alternating action of the arms. The arms may be lifted above the surface of the water.

2. Walk in water that is chest depth, emphasizing the push of the feet against the bottom. Propel the body in a horizontal position utilizing a similar action.

3. Perform the leg and arm actions simultaneously.

4. While executing each of the above, experiment with the following:
Range of joint action during force production phase.
Direction of force application.
Body surfaces applying force.
Methods of placing limbs in a position to re-apply force.
Trunk and head positions.
Breathing cycle.

a) What is the most efficient manner in which to execute the parts and the combined action? _____

_____

b) Give the reasons for deciding why certain adjustments experimented with were efficient in contributing to movement of the body. _____

E. Comparison of strokes

Select one stroke from each group below and compare and contrast your selections in relation to the points listed in Worksheet 10–3.

Group 1	Group 2
Elementary Backstroke	Front Crawl
Side Stroke	Back Crawl
Breast Stroke	Trudgeon
Side Overarm	Trudgeon Crawl
Inverted Breast Stroke	

WORKSHEET 10–3 Comparison of Strokes

Stroke:		
Body position		
Force production: arms		
Legs		
Recovery phase: arms		
Legs		
Rhythmic organization		
Important sensory cues		
Major outcomes of performance		

F. Changing direction

1. While learning to execute the tuck, pike, and/or foot-first surface dives, answer the following questions:

   a) Identify and explain the manner in which the various mechanical factors are operating. _____

   _____

   _____

   _____

   b) How do various positions of the head affect performance? _____

   _____

   c) In what situations might each of these surface dives be employed? Why? _____

   _____

   Tuck _____

   Pike _____

   Foot-first _____

WORKSHEET 10–4   Changing Direction

Position and stroke	Trials									
	1	2	3	4	5	6	7	8	9	10
Prone										
Side										
Supine										

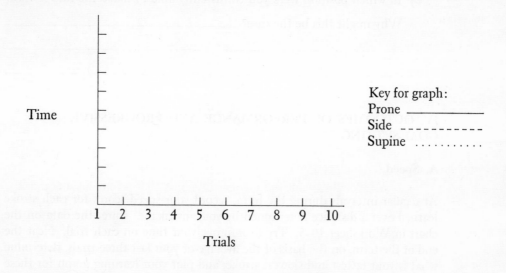

Time

Trials

Key for graph:
Prone _____
Side _ _ _ _ _ _ _ _ _ _
Supine . . . .

2. Measure the amounts of time required to reverse your direction after touching the side of the pool. Have a partner start the watch when you make contact with the edge of the pool and stop the watch when contact is lost during the pushoff phase. If you are a proficient swimmer you may wish to utilize racing turns. Have your partner start timing at the commencement of the turning action. Record your times on the chart in Worksheet 10–4. Use strokes that place the body in each of three positions: side, prone, and supine. On your chart, indicate the stroke used for each position. When you have completed all trials, plot your learning graph for each position on Worksheet 10–4.

a) Compare the similarities and differences between the curves in relation to shape. _____

_____

b) What factors contributed (or should contribute) to an improvement in performance? _____

_____

c) In which position were you consistently able to make the fastest turn? Why might this be the case? _____

_____

IV. OUTCOMES OF PERFORMANCE AND PROGRESSIVE GOAL-SETTING

A. Speed

At regular intervals during the term, record your speed scores for each stroke learned over a distance determined by your instructor. Enter the data on the chart in Worksheet 10–5. Try to improve your time on each trial. Near the end of the term, on the basis of the average of your last three trials, determine what is your fastest and slowest stroke, and plot your learning graph for these strokes on Worksheet 10–5.

a) Compare the two curves, pointing out the significant similarities and differences. _____

b) What major factors contributed to your being able to perform one stroke faster than the other? _____

_____

c) Did the same or nearly the same pattern of performance occur for similar types of strokes? If so, which strokes? _____

WORKSHEET 10–5   Record of Speed Scores

Stroke	Trial (date)										Average of last 3 trials
1.											
2.											
3.											
4.											
5.											
6.											

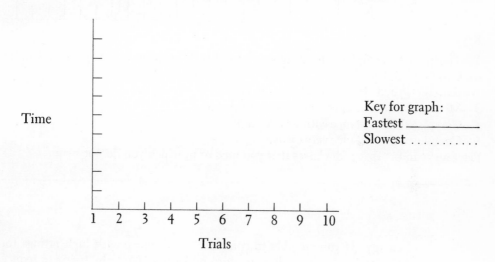

Time

Key for graph:
Fastest _____
Slowest . . . .

1 2 3 4 5 6 7 8 9 10

Trials

B. Endurance

1. During each class period swim ten (10) lengths of the pool (or other appropriate distance as designated by your instructor), using the same stroke for the entire distance. On the chart in Worksheet 10–6 record the manner in which you completed the distance, using the key that appears below the chart. As soon as you are able to rate yourself with a 4 on two successive days or a 5 on one day, switch to a stroke that requires a greater output

WORKSHEET 10–6   Record of Endurance Development

Stroke employed	Class period																							
	1	2	3	4	5	6	7	8	9	10	11	12	13	14	15	16	17	18	19	20	21	22	23	24

Key:

1—Too tired to complete the distance. (In this instance record how many lengths were completed, e.g., "1–4.")
2—Extremely tired after completion of the distance.
3—Moderately tired after completion of the distance.
4—Completed the distance with relative ease.
5—Completed the distance very easily.
Place an × in the space for classes that you miss or in which you do not swim.

of energy. If you are able to complete the distance with high ratings for all the strokes you are able to execute, add a time factor by trying to reduce the total amount of time needed to complete the task.

a) Which stroke(s) do you feel contributed most to your developing endurance? _____

b) On what did you base your opinion? _____

c) What effect if any, does the breathing phase of a stroke have on your endurance? Illustrate your answer by referring to your record. _____

2. At selected intervals during the term measure the time and distance (to the nearest foot) that you are able to swim underwater. Record the results on the chart in Worksheet 10–7. Near the end of the term, plot two learning graphs, one for time and one for distance, on Worksheet 10–7.

   a) What adjustments did you make in your stroke in order to improve

   your distance score? _____

   _____

   b) Which measure, time or distance, was the most difficult to improve?

   What factors might have contributed to this? _____

   _____

   _____

   c) From a cursory examination of the two curves, does there appear to be

   a relationship between the two factors? _____

   _____

3. Experiment with different types of leg actions while treading water, using (a) a flutter type action, (b) a scissor type action, (c) a frog type of action. Try to use a minimum of arm action.

   At selected intervals during the term tread water for two minutes, using the kick found to be most efficient for you. Try to progress through the sequence listed in Worksheet 10–8. Move up a stage when you can easily tread for two minutes at the stage on which you are working.

   a) What factor(s) is/are operating to make the task progressively more

   difficult? _____

   _____

   b) What are the similarities and differences between the three experiments

   in this section on endurance? _____

   _____

   _____

   _____

   _____

   _____

   _____

WORKSHEET 10-7   Underwater Time and Distance Record

	Trials									
	1	2	3	4	5	6	7	8	9	10
Date										
Time										
Distance										

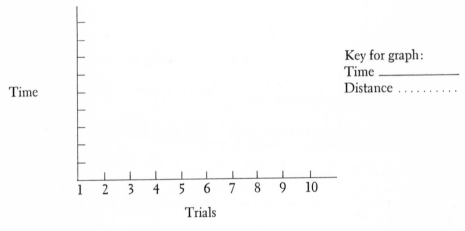

Key for graph:
Time _____
Distance . . . .

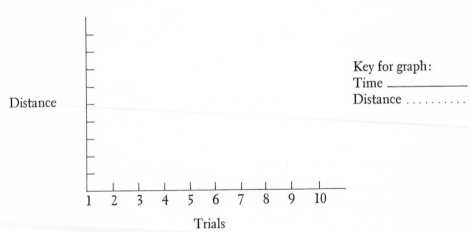

Key for graph:
Time _____
Distance . . . .

WORKSHEET 10–8   Treading Water

Record a check for each trial complete at each level. Use a 0 to indicate each trial attempted but not completed.

Sequence	Date									
1. Tread with the aid of arm action										
2. Tread without arm action, hands under the water										
3. Tread with one finger of each hand out of the water										
4. Tread with both hands out of water										
5. Tread with the forearms out of water										
6. Tread with as much of the arms out of water as possible										

V. UNDERSTANDING YOUR CAPABILITIES FOR MOVEMENT

1. Observe several students of varying body types executing a motionless back float. What factors allow some to maintain a horizontal position more easily? _____

_____

_____

2. What factors examined in Chapters 8 and 9, self-assessment and conditioning, may facilitate and/or hinder *your* ability to move in the aquatic medium. Refer to specific skills to illustrate your answers. _____

_____

_____

chapter 11
MOVEMENT BEHAVIOR
UNDER CONDITIONS
OF MINIMUM SUPPORT

One of the constant pursuits of man through time has been the attempt to discover the order of things in his natural world. He has learned to place complete faith in certain repeated phenomena: rising sun, returning spring, the effects of gravity. The movement of a human being is also a natural phenomenon and, as was discussed in Chapter 1, it is explainable to a great degree by certain characteristics of the species and our earth-world environment. We hope that by now you have discarded the notion that skill and efficiency in movement are mystical qualities possessed by some and noticeably absent in others. No matter what your present level of skillfulness, *greater* skillfulness and enjoyment can be yours through continued learning about yourself and the constant laws that underlie human movement possibilities.

In this chapter the discussion centers on moving through space with only partial support—or, momentarily, no support—for the body. One of the best ways to explore movement under these conditions is through the use of gymnastic apparatus.

The ways in which the body functions as a complex lever system have been described previously in Chapter 3. From this material we can generalize that the body lever systems may be utilized in at least four basic ways: (1) to balance weights, including that of the body itself, (2) to overcome weights or, in the present context, to build body momentum, (3) to vary the momentum potential of a given arrangement of weights, and (4) to receive momentum. We shall consider first the balancing of body weight under conditions of minimum support.

BALANCING OF BODY WEIGHT

In a lever system functioning for balance, weights must be equally distributed around (or on either side of) the fulcrum, as in the classic example of the see-saw. For our purposes, we shall describe balance and balance problems in terms of the center of gravity, line of gravity, and base of support. Certain relationships among these factors must exist if balance is to be maintained, whether one is simply walking to class or walking a tightrope over Niagara Falls.

Principle 1. The nearer the line of gravity falls to the center of the base of support, the greater the probability of maintaining balance. If an individual stands with her feet parallel and about shoulder width apart, the size of her base of support is a rectangle approximately 1½′ × 1′. With her weight evenly distributed between both feet, the line of gravity should fall in the center of the base of support and the probability of maintaining balance is maximum. If she shifts her weight far to one side, the line of gravity falls closer to the edges of the base and the chances of maintaining balance decrease. If the line of gravity falls outside the base of support, she will have to establish a new base or she will fall. (Recall Fig. 3–2.)

Principle 2. The broader the base of support, generally speaking, the better the probability of maintaining balance. The logic of this principle is immediately apparent, just as a four-legged table maintains its state of equilibrium more readily than a broom standing on end. The broom is less able to maintain stability because of the narrowness of the broom's base of support. (Recall Fig. 3–1.)

Principle 3. The probability of maintaining balance is increased when the center of gravity is lowered in relation to the base. The football center, guard, or tackle, goes into his familiar three-point stance at the line because he is difficult to knock down in that position. So, also, a person about to be hit by a wave at the seashore will crouch a little lower as the wave breaks. Many people react in this manner in similar situations—they feel "safer" a little closer to the earth. The wisdom of this reaction is consonant with the laws governing human motion.

Principle 4. The further one body segment moves away from the line of gravity, the greater the probability of losing balance, unless another segment moves to compensate for it. This can be most clearly seen, perhaps, if the body can be visualized in four quadrants: an upper left, upper right, lower left, and lower right. If an individual stretches far to her right to catch a grounder in softball, she must somehow counterbalance her strong lean downward and to the right by an adjustment in the lower *left* quadrant; otherwise she will be unable to maintain stability, straighten, and throw after catching the ball. Similarly, when a person stands on tiptoe and leans far forward to bring down a hat box from the top shelf of a closet, she usually extends one leg behind the body to counterbalance the forward lean.

From the examples just given, it may be seen that we respond automatically and efficiently to some balance-problem situations. Certain experiences wherein the body has minimum or unusual bases of support may serve, however, not only to sharpen balance skills but also to increase one's knowledge of the delicate responses the body makes in the relocation of weight for maintenance of balance during participation in vigorous movement.

Balancing over a narrow base of support

In general we have learned "balancing" in usual life tasks, and we have ceased to be aware of this never-ending function. In order to bring this basic skill to the conscious level and attempt to improve it, we can explore new and more complex balance-problem situations.

Principle 1. The relationship of the line of gravity to the base of support

Experiment A: High or low balance beam. A plumb line is dropped along an individual's approximate line of gravity as she stands with both feet on the beam and weight evenly distributed. (The plumb line is held either by another person on the beam or by a person on the floor.) The plumb line is allowed to fall forward along with the imaginary line of gravity as the individual shifts her weight toward a front-scale position. It will be seen that balance becomes more difficult as the line of gravity falls closer to the edges of the base of support. Finally, as the back foot comes off the beam, the line of gravity must bisect the new base of support (the forward foot) or balance will be lost.

Desired result 1. See Fig. 11–1.

Desired result 2. The performer will lift the non-supporting leg until it is exactly parallel to the floor. Observers can help her identify this point initially. The performer will then try to move from *the two-foot stand* to the *scale with non-supporting leg parallel to the floor* without hesitation or wavering. Note: when this is mastered, the performer is said to have a kinesthetic awareness of what "leg parallel to the floor" means.

Experiment B: Uneven parallel bars. An individual stands in a lunge position on the low bar of the unevens, holding onto the high bar. She attempts to balance on the low bar without the aid of the high bar support, never, how-

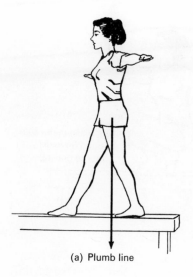
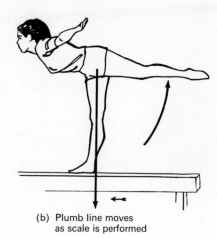

(a) Plumb line

(b) Plumb line moves
as scale is performed

Fig. 11–1.

ever, removing her hand completely from the supporting bar. To be successful, the body segments must be maintained in perfect alignment.

Principle 2. The size of the base of support

Experiment: High beam (with spotters) or low beam. After practicing pivot turns on the floor, an individual takes a regular standing position on the beam with feet about 12–18 inches apart. She completes a pivot turn on the beam. Then she places her feet as close together as possible, heels slightly elevated, and performs another pivot turn. Except in unusual circumstances, the second turn will be more difficult, principally because of the reduced size of the base of support.

Desired result. The performer works for a fairly swift turn with no abrupt torso or arm movements to facilitate balance. The often-suggested spotting hint of "looking at the end of the beam as the turn is started and then as quickly as possible focusing on the other end of the beam" is probably a helpful perceptual cue. The quick focus on the stationary object may reduce the whirling sensation from a wandering kind of focus, which takes in many objects as they pass by the performer's view.

Principle 3. The center of gravity in relation to the base

Experiment A: High beam or low beam. The pivot turns are repeated, once from a standing position and once from a squatting position. It will be found

Pivot
Turn while in the squat
position (lowered
center of gravity)

Fig. 11–2.

that the squat pivot turn is more easily controlled because of the lowered center of gravity.

Desired result. See Fig. 11–2.

Experiment B: High beam. From a sitting position astride the beam, the upper torso is extended to a front lying position on the beam. The resulting stability is brought about through the combined effects of lowering the center of gravity and broadening the base of support.

Principle 4. Body segments moving away from the line of gravity

Experiment A: Low beam. In a squatting or standing position, a rubber playground ball is bounced along side of the beam as an individual walks. The ball should first be bounced as far away from the beam as arm length will allow. The individual then repeats the walk down the length of the beam, bouncing the ball as close to the beam as possible. The second trip should be much more efficient because less body compensation is required than for the first trip.

Desired result. A completed trip down the beam will probably be impossible while the ball is bounced far away from the body. It will be possible, however, when the ball is bounced close to the beam if the performer focuses on the beam as usual and allows kinesthetic cues and peripheral vision information to guide the ball bounce.

Experiment B: Uneven parallel bars. An individual assumes a swan balance position on the low bar of the unevens. She then attempts to raise the head

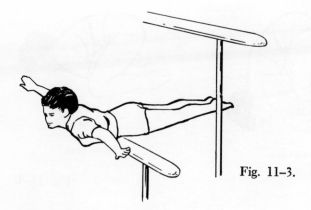

Fig. 11–3.

and shoulders slightly without moving the rest of her body. Her legs and hips must drop slightly with this movement or balance will be lost.

Desired result. See Fig. 11–3.

Balancing in an inverted position

Balancing in an inverted position will be defined here as a relatively static pose or posture wherein body weight is supported by the hands, or a combined base formed by the head and hands. Except for the occasional practitioner of yoga, inverted poses are generally avoided in our society and even associated with rather disagreeable sensations. It is interesting to note, however, that much of this response is probably the result of learning and experience. The problems of balancing are quite similar whether on feet or hands. Theoretically, we could probably teach little children to walk on their hands much more easily than is usually believed. "What if" speculations are amusing, and the picture of an upside-down society is no exception. At any rate the important point is that the same *principles* apply in balancing, no matter what the position of the body.

Principle 1. The relationship of the line of gravity to the base of support.

Experiment: An individual kicks up to a hand-stand position against a wall, with a spotter lifting and holding her hips. She can lean to the left or right a considerable distance and still have her line of gravity well within the limits of the base of support. She will notice, however, that the slightest lean away from the wall brings her down from the inverted balance! This is the immediate effect when the line of gravity falls outside the base of support.

Tripod base   Tip-up base

Fig. 11–4.

Principle 2. The size of the base of support

Experiment: An individual performs the tripod (base of support: hands and head) and the tip-up (base includes hands only) (see Fig. 11–4). Compare the relative sizes and shapes of the two bases. Which requires more muscular effort to maintain?

Principle 3. The center of gravity in relation to the base

Experiment: An individual performs a tripod. How high is the approximate center of gravity above the base of support? The same individual performs a head-stand, with or without assistance from a spotter. The base of support is the same but how high is the new center of gravity above the base?

Principle 4. Body segments moving away from the line of gravity

Experiment A: An individual performs a head-stand in tuck position and in pike position. The latter requires much more muscular effort and control. Why?

Experiment B: The individual hangs by her knees from the low bar of the unevens, hands on the bar in reverse grip. The knees are then moved away from the bar so that the individual hangs by the hands in a "skin-the-cat" position. With the knees tucked in to the chest, all of the body parts are fairly close to the center of gravity and the balanced hang is not difficult to maintain. If, however, the legs are extended into a pike position, the balanced hang is much more difficult to maintain. It requires a good deal of muscular effort to compensate for the weight of the legs extended away from the line of gravity.

BUILDING MOMENTUM AND VARYING MOMENTUM POTENTIAL

This section of the chapter deals with the body lever systems as they function to create or maintain force and project the body through space.

Momentum production in the *vertical* and *diagonal* (upward-forward) planes

Let us represent this type of force production with the trampoline bounce and simple vaulting moves. The mechanics involved in force production are similar in both cases, since it is a variation in weight placement that primarily accounts for the difference in direction of body flight.

Principle 5. The angle of body flight is determined by the placement of the center of gravity in relation to the supporting base at the moment of take-off.

Experiment: Trampoline. The performer assumes a stance so that her line of gravity is vertical, and begins to bounce on the trampoline. If she is able to maintain this alignment, she will bounce up and down in about the same spot. If she drops her head forward (to look at her feet, for instance), then the line of gravity shifts forward and the body flight becomes forward and upward rather than simply upward.

An explanation of the above, the knowledge of which provides one of the keys to creating momentum, is revealed in Newton's Law of Action-Reaction, which we restate below as a basic principle of human movement.

Principle 6. For every action there is an equal and opposite reaction. In the trampoline example given above, the slight inclination of the body made the feet and legs press against the mat in a downward and backward direction, thus projecting the body forward and upward by the equal, yet opposite, reaction.

Experiment A: Trampoline. The performer executes a seat-drop. If alignment is maintained so that the heels, legs, hips all strike the mat at the same time with the head and upper torso extended directly above the hips, the rebound from the mat will be very nearly vertical. If the legs and feet strike first, the rebound will be upward and backward and standing position will not be regained. Again, a kinesthetic sense, regarding when the legs are piked "enough but not too much," must be developed.

Experiment B: Side horse or buck. In most vaults, the performer wants to build as much height as she can manage and still perform the vault in a mechanically correct fashion. This height gives her the advantage of *time*: time to perform the complex series of movements demanded in some vaults, and time that will allow her body to travel farther in the air before gravity causes her to end the vault. This maximum height and maximum distance is achieved, principally, through rapid extension of the hips, knee, and ankle joints, which results in a strong leg drive against the floor. The torso has a slight forward lean at the moment of take-off (the center of gravity is also slightly forward of the base of support) and the equal and opposite reaction from the floor (and from the horse as the hands and arms cause rebound) propels the individual over the horse. There are many possible body positions one might assume during the flight phase of a vault, but the take-off remains basically the same.

Rotational momentum production

A force applied away from the center of gravity of any freely movable object will cause that object to rotate. Force imparted to the upper or lower portions of the human body bring about the rotation of the forward roll or somersault. Force toward the sides of the body brings about the rotations that occur in the dancers' pirouette and in the swivel hips on the trampoline.

Principle 7. Rotary motion is produced by force applied away from the center of gravity of an object.

Experiment A: Rotation, uneven bars. Although there are many floor moves involving vertical rotation, perhaps the most clear example would begin with a front balance from the low bar of the unevens, hands in a reverse grip. The performer simply drops her head and tucks her legs. The rotation is automatic. Most individuals will not get all the way around because the hips drop away from the bar and the body lever becomes so long that it slows itself down by its own weight.

    Questions: In the front balance, approximately where is the body center of gravity? What is the force applied that starts the body rotating around the bar?

Experiment B: Rotation, trampoline. Let us assume that the performer wishes to rotate a half-turn in a clockwise direction around her right shoulder. At the height of a bounce she will fling her left arm toward her right shoulder, turn her head toward the right and rotate her hips toward the right. This uneven action toward one side of the body will begin the desired rotation. The *process* of rotation-building would be approximately the same if full or one-and-a-half turns were desired.

Pendular momentum production

When the body hangs, or swings, suspended from some stable support, it behaves like a pendulum. Gravity greatly affects the force required for the movement of a pendulum; it increases the force of the pendulum *downswing* and decreases the force of the *upswing.* How can we take advantage of this fact as we swing from a rope, a horizontal ladder, or the high bar of the unevens?

Experiences: Uneven Bars

1. As the performer hangs suspended from the high bar, what are the various ways in which force could be applied to begin a pendular swing?
2. Will the performer go on swinging indefinitely without exerting muscular effort? What are the factors which slow and eventually stop the swing?
3. How can the performer vary the length of the body as it acts as a pendulum? What kinds of changes in speed of swing occur?
4. How would the performer move in order to build as big a swing as possible?

There is another unique and interesting facet of pendular movement. There is a split second when gravity has neutralized the momentum of the backswing, and just before the downswing begins, when the body is experienced as almost weightless. One can empathize momentarily with our astronauts as the "sinking feeling in the stomach" quickly passes. This is the moment, also, when the individual can safely drop off the apparatus without difficulty, for there is no horizontal momentum and a vertical drop may be executed.

Experiment: As the performer swings easily, she will dismount (by dropping away from the bar) at the zero point of her backswing. She may also try to reverse one hand on the bar at the zero point in her backswing and continue to swing easily with the hands in a mixed grip.

We have been considering the general way in which momentum is imparted to the body and also the directions in which this momentum may be channeled. We must also deal with the development of varying degrees of momentum. What factors affect the *amount* of momentum created by gravity and/or muscular effort? Three main ones may be identified.

Principle 8. The greater the number of body segments involved, generally speaking, the greater the momentum production.

Experiments: Trampoline

A. Bounce with ankles and knees locked and arms at sides.
B. Bounce with full flexion and extension of hip and knee joint but feet flat, arms at sides.
C. Bounce with full flexion and extension of ankle, knee, and hips. Arms at sides.
D. Bounce as in C above, but with full arm circles.

Principle 9. The longer the body segment or lever involved, the greater the momentum production, if a minimum speed is maintained.

Experiment: Uneven bars. See Experiences 3 and 4 in the introduction to this section.

Principle 10. The greater the speed of the body segments, generally speaking, the greater will be the momentum imparted.

Experiment: Trampoline. The swivel hips on the trampoline demands a certain degree of speed in body movement. The performer moves from a seat drop in one direction to a half-turn, followed by another seat drop.

In most efficient performance, the individual will move from the seat drop to a vertically extended position above the trampoline bed, will make a half-turn (as described in Experiment B under Principle 7), and then move into the second seat drop.

All too often, a novice performer will attempt to make the half-turn with the body still in an L-shape or pike position. The length of the body lever in this instance makes the maintenance of minimum speed for accomplishing the half-turn next to impossible and it will not be completed.

RECEIVING MOMENTUM

The final section of this chapter deals chiefly with controlling or diminishing momentum. This is a topic that will be dealt with more fully by your instructor in conjunction with the teaching of traditional sport activities. A major concern in the context of this chapter is that of landing safely from a height.

Principle 11. The more gradually momentum is diminished, the less the likelihood of injury.

Experiment: Jumping or dropping from a height. Remember that momentum is imparted to the body by rapid extension of the ankle, knee, and hip. Flexion of these segments bring about a gradual reduction of momentum. When jumping or dropping from a height, the individual should land on the ball of the foot, let the heel roll down to the floor accompanied by ankle, knee, and hip flexion. This segmental action extends the *moment of impact* over a longer period of time and more space than does a flat-footed, locked knee landing and is, therefore, much safer. The diminishing effect of flexion on momentum can also be seen in the "breaking of the bounce" on the trampoline, or when a performer flexes the upper spine in performing a knee drop.

SUMMARY

This chapter has enumerated eleven principles descriptive of body motion where the complex lever systems are functioning to: (1) balance body weight; (2) build and direct body momentum; (3) vary the amount of body momentum, and (4) decrease body momentum. Experiments are suggested to clarify these principles.

SUGGESTED READING

BROER, MARION, *Efficiency of Human Movement*, Second Edition. Philadelphia: W. B. Saunders Company, 1966

COOPER, JOHN M., AND RUTH B. GLASSOW, *Kinesiology*. St. Louis: The C. V. Mosby Company, 1963 (Chapters 10 and 14)

DRURY, BLANCHE J., AND ANDREA B. SCHMID, *Gymnastics for Women*, Revised Edition. Palo Alto, California: The National Press, 1965

WELLS, KATHARINE F., *Kinesiology*. Philadelphia: W. B. Saunders Company, 1958 (Chapters 1, 17, 19, 20)

chapter 12
MOVEMENT AND RHYTHM

Rhythm is a reality of human experience that challenges common understanding because it exists at the perceptual level, and perception, of course, is a unique organization of sensations having true meaning for the perceiver only. In this chapter we shall attempt to identify some commonalities of rhythmic experience—particularly proprioceptive rhythmic experience—so that your movement activities may be enriched and improved by cognizance of, and response to, the many rhythms that occur in daily life.

RHYTHM AND TIME

In the broadest sense, we can say that rhythm is an organization of events. A succession of regularly recurring events, for instance sound events, marks the passage of time. The tick of a clock, the drone of a ship's foghorn, the drip of a water faucet, the beat of any steady pattern measures time into intervals. Awareness of time, then, may be based upon the perception of sounds and the intervals between sounds. A sound event that is heard and then recalled during a succeeding interval is perceived as an event of the past. The moment of receiving the sound sensation is perceived as present. Anticipation of the next sound event (during an interval of silence) enables the listener to conceive of future time. Organized sound events thus help an individual to distinguish his own existence in time from infinity.

Further temporal differentiation is possible when accent, i.e., emphasis, is used to group successive events into units. With sound events, the accent normally marks the beginning of a unit. The units so created are of a higher order of rhythmic structure because they are more comprehensible than the relatively unorganized succession of events cited previously. Due to a compulsion to comprehend and to order events, individuals will subjectively "add"

Fig. 12–1. An example of visual rhythm: windows of a building. (Photo by A. Devaney, Inc.)

accent and effect grouping if this is not done for them. It is natural to want to recognize and repeat the organization of events, and accent makes it easier for a person to recognize and reproduce a particular rhythmic structure.

TYPES OF RHYTHMIC EXPERIENCES

Different kinds of rhythmic experiences may be categorized according to the manner in which they are perceived. For example, *auditory* rhythmic structures are organizations of *time* events, namely sounds. As described previously, when the sounds are organized into units, by means of accents, the listener can perceive wholeness and repetition. It is then possible for the individual to recognize the rhythmic organization of the sound events and to reproduce this organization himself.

A second type of rhythmic experience is *visual*. Visual rhythmic structures are organizations of *space* events: animals, objects, or materials that can be seen. Again, the presence of accent serves to lend rhythmic organization to the events. The representation of a modern building illustrates the point (see Fig. 12–1). The events seen here are materials: sheets of glass and steel girders. The steel girders provide accent and mark the otherwise continuous glass into units.

A third type of rhythmic experience is *proprioceptive*. Here we are concerned with an organization of body-movement events. Movement is unique among rhythmic experiences because it is a *space-time* organization of events. Body movement, for example, involves the displacement of a body segment; the movement, or displacement, is from one point to another through *space*, and the displacement consumes a certain amount of *time*. Although the space and time components may be discussed separately, during the movement itself they are inseparable. This is why we use the term "space-time." The accents that lend rhythmic organization to human movement are the various force phases that occur during the execution of a movement pattern.

QUALITIES OF MOVEMENT

There are three primary qualities that may be associated with any human movement: a swing quality (gravity and ballistic), a sustained quality, and a percussive quality. Of the three, the swing quality occurs most frequently. This is probably explained by the mechanical structure of the body; the ball-and-socket joints of the shoulder and hip allow limbs to swing easily in a forward and backward direction.

Swing movements. Bowling and gymnastics are examples of activities that utilize the gravity swing. Force, either internal (muscular) or external (gravitational), initiates and sustains movement in space-time. The initiating force and the movement in space-time itself generate a specific momentum that may be transferred to another body segment or object (see Diagram 12-1). In bowling, muscular force initiates the forward and downward movement. The movement accelerates as the bowling ball and arm react to the pull of gravity. Momentum carries the arm to the height of the backswing; there is a slight pause (direction is changed from backward to forward during this point of near-zero motion), and muscular force initiates the forward swing. Gravity again increases momentum to a point of maximum acceleration (the force phase, or accent), and there the ball is released. The arm, however, continues on to the natural termination of the swinging arc. This natural termination of a movement after impact or point of release is ordinarily known as follow-through.

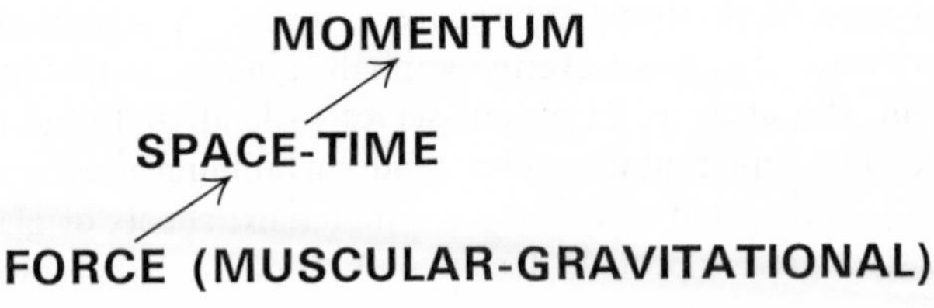

MOMENTUM

⤴

SPACE-TIME

⤴

FORCE (MUSCULAR-GRAVITATIONAL)

Diagram 12–1.

To summarize: gravity swings are characterized by an initiating force, a giving way to gravity, a second initiating force as direction is changed, and another giving way to gravity. The bowling swing is diagrammed in Fig. 12–2, with movements counted 1–6. A 1-2-3 count could, of course, be applied to both the backward and the forward swing. For purpose of discussion, however, a six-count breakdown is clearer.

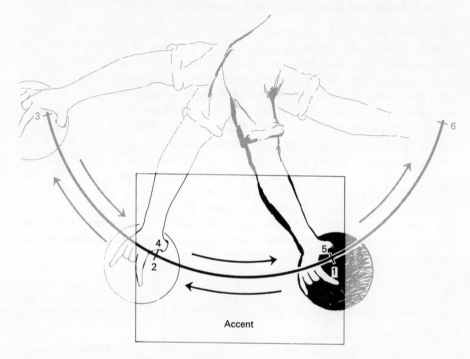

Fig. 12–2. Rhythm of a bowling swing.

It should be pointed out that whenever a count is applied to movement, movement is actually initiated and executed *before* the count and, in fact, frequently terminates on the count. For example, in our diagram of a bowling swing we see that counts 1 and 4 occur, not at the initiation of a given movement, but at the lower phase of the arc that represents the movement. When verbalizing this count, it may be helpful to say, "and 1, 2, 3, and 4, 5, 6." There is a period of acceleration and one of deceleration during each group of three counts. The accent occurs at the point of maximum acceleration— count 1 on the backswing and count 4 on the forward swing. Release of the ball should occur at or around count 4, since this is the most forceful phase of the forward movement.

Several interpretations of the ballistic swing can be found in the literature, but it will be defined here as follows. A ballistic swing is a swing initiated by forceful muscular action that produces rapid acceleration. The accent occurs at the beginning of the swing, and there is relatively constant speed until contact or point of release, then deceleration.

Considering the *forward* portion of the movement *only*, most throwing, striking, and kicking movements represent ballistic swings. (The backward portion of the movement, the preparatory action, has a sustained quality—see below). Examples of sport skills employing a ballistic swing are various throws, tennis and badminton strokes, batting, and golf.

Sustained movement. Sustained movement is characterized by constant speed, which is accomplished by an equalized release of energy. No accent occurs; the movement flows smoothly, evenly, continuously. This type of movement is often used in contemporary dance for expressive purposes, but it is also found in combination with other types of movement in sport skills.

The examples of ballistic-swing skills just cited employ a backswing that is essentially sustained. An overarm throw executed with the intent of maximum speed is a case in point. The thrower initiates a downward and backward preparatory action (wind-up) that places the muscles on stretch and readies them for vigorous contraction when forward motion is initiated. The backswing has a sustained quality, but from the instant when forward motion begins, the movement is ballistic in nature. Forward movement is initiated by vigorous muscular effort (the force phase of the movement) and there is relatively constant speed until point of release, then deceleration during follow-through (see Fig. 12–3).

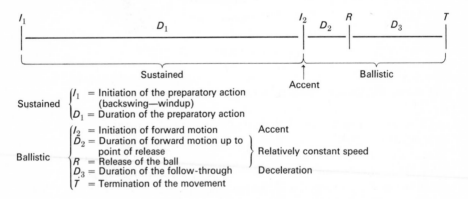

Fig. 12–3. Relative time relationship between phases of the overarm throw.

Percussive movement. In percussive movement there is rapid acceleration toward an accent that occurs at the *end* of the pattern. There is little or no follow-through; rather, there is an abrupt energy release, marking the end of the movement. Dancers, especially contemporary dancers, may use percussive movements (as well as sustained movements) for expressive purposes. How-

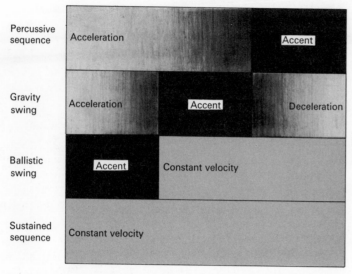

Fig. 12–4. Rhythmic organization of various movement sequences.

ever, the movement may also be observed in such activities as hammering a nail, hitting a punching bag, or attempting a touché in fencing.

In Fig. 12–4 we compare the rhythmical organization of percussive, swing, and sustained movement sequences. Accent in these sequences may be a result of muscular effort or gravity.

ORGANIZATION OF RHYTHMIC STRUCTURES

The organization of events into a rhythmic structure is accomplished by several devices. Although these devices tend to be associated strictly with auditory rhythmic experiences, particularly with music, they apply to the ordering of all events—auditory, visual, and proprioceptive. The common devices are:

1) Underlying beat—steady, continuing basic count.

2) Accent—special emphasis; increased force.

3) Measure—small units that are made evident by accent.

4) Phrase—larger units that have a feeling of wholeness and completeness in themselves.

5) Syncopation—the temporary displacement of accent onto a beat where it is unexpected.

Chart 12–1 illustrates the cross-situational meaning of these terms, so that you may be helped to understand rhythm and these rhythmical devices in more than a musical sense.

CHART 12-1   Rhythmic Devices in the Various Perceptual Modes

Device	Proprioceptive	Auditory	Visual
	Example: *Bowling swing*	Example: *Waltz music*	Example: *Brick building*
Underlying beat	1–2–3–4–5–6	1–2–3, 1–2–3, etc.	Bricks (1–2–3–4–5 . . .)
Accent	On counts 1 and 4	On count 1	At windows (a space inserted in rows of bricks)
Measure	Backswing (1–2–3) or forward swing (4–5–6)	A single 1–2–3 count	Window and the rows of bricks leading to the next window
Phrase	Complete swing	Two or more measures that are grouped together by the composer as a larger unit	Series of above
Syncopation	Release other than on count 4	Accent on count 2 or 3	Window in unexpected place

SELF-DETERMINED RHYTHMIC ORGANIZATION

In movement activity, rhythmic organization may be determined by the performer, or it may occur in response to a superimposed rhythmic structure. The qualities of movement just considered may appear in either case. With self-determined rhythmic organization the performer is free to create a rhythmic pattern that is unique to himself, without conforming to external stimuli. Much movement of daily life falls in this category. In putting on a coat or in boarding a bus, for example, each person organizes space-time in his own unique way. Thus each individual has his own particular rhythmic structure for any given movement task.

Since all movement occurs in space-time and has certain characteristics of force, it may be helpful at this point to take a closer look at the elements associated with space, time, and force in movement.

The elements of the *space* component are:

a) *Direction.* The path of the movement in the horizontal dimension and the relationship of the body to that path.

b) *Level.* The point in the vertical dimension at which the movement occurs.

c) *Magnitude* or *range.* The amount of space used by the movement in both the horizontal and vertical dimensions.

The elements of the *time* component are:

a) *Speed.* The rate of motion of a body, body segment, or object.

b) *Duration.* The amount of time consumed by a movement and the length of the interval between movements. Duration may vary or remain constant, and thus result in "uneven" or "even" movement patterns (see discussion below).

The elements of the *force* component are:

a) *Intensity.* The degree of force produced. Accent represents a high degree of intensity.

b) *Tension.* The tension-relaxation status of muscles or muscle groups.

All movement activities, daily tasks, sports, dance, gymnastics, aquatics, and the locomotor and nonlocomotor movements upon which they are based may be analyzed according to their spatial-temporal organization and specific force characteristics. In the context of rhythm, locomotor movements are commonly classified as "even" or "uneven." The walk, run, leap, jump, and hop are locomotor movements based upon an even rhythmic pattern; that is, the duration of the intervals between "beats" is equal. In the slide, gallop, and skip, by contrast, two or more locomotor movements that are normally even are combined into uneven rhythmic patterns; that is, there are unequal time intervals between beats.

We stated previously that in self-determined rhythmical movement, each person organizes space-time in his own unique way. Assuming that he is able to recognize the space-time and force characteristics of a given movement, he tends to reproduce those characteristics by moving his limbs in a particular direction, at a specific level, through a certain amount of space and at a given speed and degree of intensity. Thus he moves with a rhythmic pattern unique to himself, and does so consistently. It follows then, that consistency in movement skills depends in part on one's ability to recognize and reproduce the rhythmic structure of the desired action. For example, if a performer has recognized the rhythmic organization of the forehand drive in tennis, and if he can reproduce it at will, other factors being equal, he is consistent in his forehand drive.

DANCES

Let us shift our attention now to movement that occurs in response to an imposed rhythmic structure, one produced by a source external to the performer. In such a case, a stimulus is presented and the performer must match his movement to the rhythmic structure of the stimulus. Dance is an obvious example of this type of rhythmic response.

When a person is responding to an imposed rhythmic pattern, such as dance accompaniment, he must organize his movement in space-time in a very prescribed way that may not be in harmony with his natural way of moving. One's enjoyment of this movement activity is frequently in direct proportion to his ability to make an accurate rhythmic response. Some people find the task so frustrating that they simply avoid these movement situations. For those who are able to perceive the stimulus accurately and make a precise response, however, the joy derived from the experience is very great indeed.

Folk dance

For the most part, folk dances developed in the past among peasant classes throughout the world. Individuals now, as then, identify closely with the groups of which they are a part. It is natural then, that cultural interests and traditions are expressed in the movement activities of its people. Folk dances have themes based upon occupation, courtship, religion, conflict, and celebration. The dances are based upon the locomotor movements belonging universally to everyone, and so participation is possible for all.

Rhythmically, the basic folk dance steps are simply locomotor movements of long or short duration organized into an even or uneven pattern.

Schottische. The schottische combines three steps and a hop in an even rhythmic pattern (see Diagram 12–2). An even pattern has been defined as one in which the intervals between beats are equal. Each movement is also of the same duration. The underlying beat is shown along the bottom of the

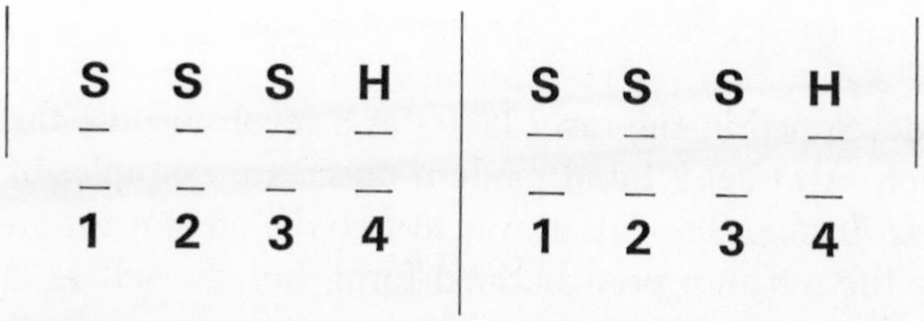

S	S	S	H		S	S	S	H
1	2	3	4		1	2	3	4

Diagram 12–2. Rhythmic structure of the schottische.

diagram, and the movements composing the rhythmic pattern are represented along the top. The movements are: step forward on the right foot, step forward on the left, step forward on the right, and hop on the right. The pattern is then repeated with the left foot leading. The cue words, then, are *step, step, step, hop*.

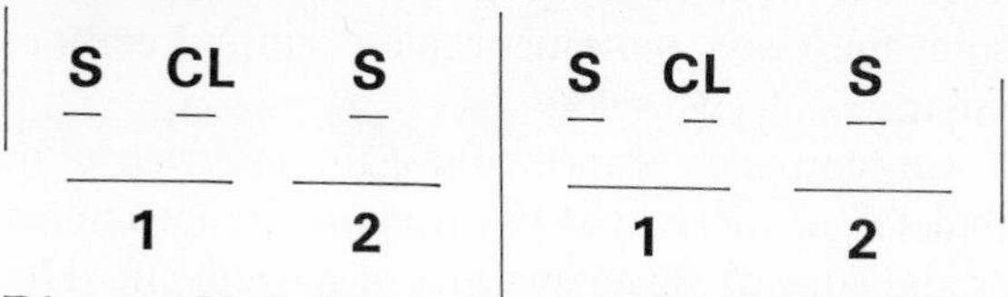

S	CL	S		S	CL	S
1		2		1		2

Diagram 12–3. Rhythmic structure of the two-step.

Two-step. The two-step combines three steps in a step, together, step pattern. The rhythmic pattern is uneven in that the movements and the intervals between movements are unequal in duration. The underlying beat and the rhythmic pattern are represented in Diagram 12–3. The movements are: step forward on the right foot, step on the ball of the left foot (beside the right heel), and step forward again on the right foot. The pattern is then repeated with the left foot leading. The cue words, therefore, are *step, close, step*.

Polka. The polka combines a hop and a two-step in an uneven rhythmic pattern. Diagram 12–4 illustrates the long and short quality of the movements in the rhythmic pattern and how they correspond to the underlying beat. The movements are: hop on the right foot, then perform a two-step with the left foot leading. The pattern is then repeated beginning with a hop on the left foot, and a two-step with the right foot leading. The cue words, therefore, are: *hop, step, close, step*.

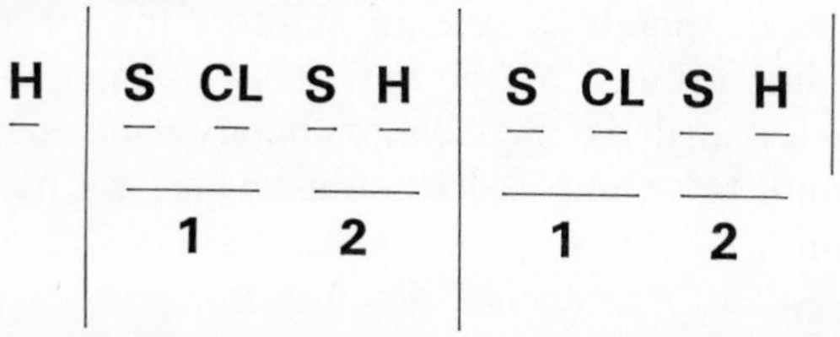

H		S	CL	S	H		S	CL	S	H
		1		2			1		2	

Diagram 12–4. Rhythmic structure of the polka.

Contemporary dance

Contemporary dance was developed in the early 1900's as a revolt against the formal restraint of the ballet. Abstract art and modern music are examples of similar rebellions in other art forms. The intent was to free the creator for an expression of the self—not the self in a prestructured form, but the self as it could structure form. All of us—whether we be painters, musicians, dancers, or simply individuals—have feelings and ideas that we seek to express. Whether our communicative avenue be canvas, instrument, or movement, we take satisfaction in having externalized what was innermost in our being.

In contemporary dance the choreographer is free to express himself. He does this through his selection of movements and their organization into sequence and pattern. A dancer may be his own choreographer, or he may be simply a performer. If he does not wish to choreograph, his only way to express himself is through someone else's movement ideas—interpretation, as in acting, is his only expression.

As students learn about contemporary dance and gain experience in moving they develop a "vocabulary" of movement based upon the locomotor and nonlocomotor movements and control of the qualities of movement. The student must discipline himself to acquire this vocabulary of movement, for it is as essential to the dancer as that of color, form, and line is to the painter and that of melody, rhythm, and harmony is to the musician. As we have previously noted, all three of these art forms share common elements, and full aesthetic appreciation is dependent on an understanding of, and sensitivity to, the interrelationships of these elements.

But once the dancer is prepared in fundamentals—that is, paradoxically, once he is disciplined—he is freed. He has all the vocabulary with which to express himself, should he desire to do so. Nothing is superimposed, unless by his own choice. For example, he may choose to respond in any of several ways to his accompaniment. He may respond rhythmically to the accompaniment (as in folk dance); he may move in contrast to the accompaniment; he may move without regard for the accompaniment; or he may move and have an accompanist follow him.

This fact leads us to the concept that in contemporary dance, as in all movement activities, rhythm arises from the movement itself, rather than from accompanying music. That is, rhythm is not synonymous with music or other forms of accompaniment; it is, primarily, an element of *movement*. Music is, in fact, an organization of sounds to give an auditory illusion of movement, and may have been first inspired by the movement of man and the movement in nature. In the last analysis, then, contemporary dance may *not* fall in the category of response to an imposed stimulus, where we have placed it for purposes of discussion.

EXTERNAL STIMULI AND RHYTHMIC ORGANIZATION

The question might now be asked, "How can a person make an accurate rhythmic response to an external stimulus?" Although the entire process is one of great complexity, it may be reduced to a simple, three-step procedure.

First, the individual must *attend* perceptually to the stimulus. The more sense modes he can utilize, that is, the more cues he can gather, the more complete his information will be. Secondly, while he is "paying attention" to the stimulus the individual must formulate a perceptual *awareness* of the underlying beat and the rhythmic pattern. And third, once he has perceived the rhythmic organization, he must *anticipate* the next stimulus. Anticipation is essential to the ability to respond precisely to an imposed stimulus. This is obvious when one considers the task of walking "in time" to music. All movement occurs before the beat itself. That is, the movement occurs during the interval between beats, and terminates on the beat. If one can anticipate when the beat is going to occur and use space-time accordingly, the task is not difficult. To summarize: Attention, awareness, and anticipation are essential in any movement activity where rhythm is imposed from a source external to the mover.

It is not always possible to maintain the same rhythmic organization for a basic movement pattern. Consider how a person must modify his natural walking or stepping pattern in the following situations: (a) getting into a self-operating elevator, (b) stepping into a revolving door when others are in it, (c) getting on and off an escalator.

Weather conditions, facilities, and equipment have decided effects upon the rhythmic organization of movement in sports. Golfers and baseball pitchers make space-time and force adjustments when hitting or throwing against a strong wind. Similar adaptations are made by tennis players when changing from clay or asphalt courts to grass courts where the ball rebounds to a lesser degree. The ball itself may impose an alteration in the rhythmic organization of the movement pattern due to its particular resiliency. Reflect for a moment upon the different response a player would make to a brand new tennis ball and the response he would necessarily make to an old, worn one. If the ball has lost its resiliency (is "dead"), you get some of the "grass court effect." The degree of tension on the racket strings also tends to impose some space-time and force modifications. In comparison with a player using a tightly strung racket, the player with a loosely strung racket must exert greater muscular force during the initiation of the ballistic phase of the movement in order to serve or drive the ball with great velocity.

Opponents may be intentionally or unintentionally responsible for causing a performer to adjust the rhythmic organization of his movement pattern. To go back for a moment to the game of tennis, suppose that an opponent runs to the net and volleys the ball for an exceptionally quick return. The other player then must make a hurried response that is significantly different in its space-time and force organization than it would otherwise have been.

Players are frequently at a disadvantage when their natural rhythmic pattern is upset by an opponent or opponents. Coaches of team sports are very aware of this phenomenon and may be heard to say, "We won because we made them play our kind of game." This comment usually means that the victorious team forced their opponents into a "team rhythm" that was unnatural. That is, they imposed their own rhythm of play, usually by slowing down or speeding up the action of the game, as is often the case in basketball. The same strategy is employed in individual sports, and with similar results, except that it is easier for one or two people to adjust to the change of rhythm than it is for many interacting players to do so.

CONCLUSION

In our natural universe most events are organized and most are repeated; therefore, it is basically a rhythmic universe. The same is true of our man-made environment, probably due to man's compulsion for order, sequence, and repetition of that sequence—or, if you will, because of his compulsion to be in harmony with nature, with the "natural" way of things. The world turns rhythmically on its axis and in most parts of the world we have a more or less even pattern of night and day; the tide ebbs and flows; water evaporates and falls; the seasons come and go; life commences, life ends. An individual's life system is similarly cyclical. Man is active, man rests; man inhales and exhales rhythmically; the heart beats a steady pattern. We are a product of our structured, repetitive universe and of our own life systems. Therefore, man likes, man needs, man must have organization and repetition of that organization—rhythm. To the extent that he moves rhythmically, to the extent that he has perceptual sensitivity to all rhythm, to that extent does he experience the aesthetic joy of harmonious relationship between his internal and external environment.

SUMMARY

1. Rhythm is an organization of events that can be recognized and reproduced. The three kinds of rhythmical experiences, categorized according to the manner in which they are perceived, are auditory, visual, and proprioceptive. In the proprioceptive experience we are concerned with the space-time organization of movement events.
2. Human movements may be classified according to their particular rhythmic quality. There are three main qualities of movement: swing (gravity and ballistic), sustained, and percussive.

3. Rhythmic movement organization may be self-determined, i.e., the performer creates his own rhythmic pattern without conforming to external stimuli, or it may occur in response to a superimposed rhythmic structure. In order to make an accurate response to an imposed stimulus the performer must attend perceptually to the stimulus, formulate an awareness of the rhythmic organization of the stimulus, and anticipate successive occurrences of the stimulus.

4. Whenever events are organized in space, in time, or in space-time, and provided that the organization of events can be recognized and repeated, there is rhythm.

SUGGESTED READING

COHEN, SELMA JEANNE (ed.), *The Modern Dance: Seven Statements of Belief.* Middletown, Conn.: Wesleyan University Press, 1965

H'DOUBLER, MARGARET, *Dance, A Creative Art Experience.* New York: F. S. Crofts and Company, 1940

LLOYD, MARGARET, *The Borzoi Book of Modern Dance.* New York: Alfred A. Knopf, 1949

LABORATORY EXPERIMENTS

I. LOCOMOTOR AND NONLOCOMOTOR MOVEMENTS

Concept 1. There are five even and three uneven locomotor movements.

Concept 2. There are twelve basic nonlocomotor movements.

Concept 3. Efficiency in the performance of locomotor and nonlocomotor movements is dependent on the following:

A. An understanding of their rhythmical organization

   1) Space
      a) Direction
      b) Level
      c) Magnitude or range

   2) Time
      a) Speed
      b) Duration

.   3) Force
         a) Intensity
         b) Tension

B. Adherence to principles of equilibrium
      1) Base of support
      2) Center of gravity of the body
      3) Line of gravity

C. Utilization of techniques of force production, control of momentum, and force reduction
      1) Newton's second law of motion: force equals mass times acceleration
      2) Newton's third law: every action has an equal and opposite reaction
      3) Sequential use of body levers in force production and reduction
      4) Space-time relationships in producing and reducing force
      5) Base of support when producing and reducing force
      6) Center of gravity when producing and reducing force
      7) Line of gravity when producing and reducing force

Experiments

1. The five even and seven uneven locomotor movements are listed below. Perform each of them with self-determined rhythmical organization, then analyze them according to the understandings listed under Concept 3.
      a) Even locomotor movements: walk, run, leap, jump, hop
      b) Uneven locomotor movements: slide, gallop, skip

2. The twelve basic nonlocomotor movements are listed below. Perform each of them with self-determined rhythmical organization, then analyze them according to the understandings listed under Concept 3.

      Nonlocomotor movements: swing, sway; pull, push; twist, turn; fall, rise; bend, stretch; strike, dodge

3. Perform combinations of locomotor and nonlocomotor movements with self-determined rhythmical organization.

II. RHYTHMIC RESPONSES TO AN IMPOSED STIMULUS

Concept. Attention, awareness, and anticipation are essential to making an accurate rhythmic response to an imposed stimulus.

Experiments

1. Perform locomotor and nonlocomotor movements, separately and in combination, to a stimulus that is increasingly more complex:
      a) Rhythmic pattern selected and produced (by clapping or percussive instrument) by the performer

b) Rhythmic pattern selected and produced (by clapping or percussive instrument) by another person

c) Music

2. When moving to music, phase out the volume until sound is not audible; continue moving, attempting to maintain the rhythm, and then increase the volume to see whether the task was accomplished. Success will indicate an internalization of the rhythmical organization of the stimulus in place of reliance upon external auditory cues.

3. Perform nonlocomotor movements, using hand apparatus such as Indian clubs, wands, ropes, hoops, scarfs, and balls to assist in developing proprioceptive awareness of the rhythmical organization of the movement.

III. VARIATIONS IN SPACE-TIME AND FORCE

Concept. Locomotor and nonlocomotor movements can be modified by making variations in space-time and force.

Experiments

1. Self-determined rhythmical organization: Perform the basic locomotor and nonlocomotor movements, varying each one according to the elements of the components of space-time and force (see Section I, Concept 3).

2. Superimposed rhythmical organization:
   a) Perform the basic locomotor and nonlocomotor movements making space-time and force variations imposed by another person (by verbal command or percussive instrument).
   b) Perform the basic locomotor and nonlocomotor movements making space-time and force variations imposed by music of differing tempos, moods, and structures.

IV. DEVICES OF RHYTHMIC ORGANIZATION

Concept. Special devices are employed in the rhythmic organization of events. These devices are: underlying beat, accent, measure, phrase, and syncopation.

Experiments

1. Listen to a simple musical structure and identify the rhythmic devices listed above.
   a) Using a notation system similar to that representing the folk dance steps and the overarm throw, illustrate the rhythmic organization of the musical structure, including the devices just identified.
   b) Make a nonlocomotor response to this organization.
   c) Make a locomotor response to this organization.

2. Look at a photograph or real object and identify the rhythmic devices.
   a) Using a notation system, illustrate the rhythmic organization of the visual stimulus, including the devices just identified.
   b) Make a nonlocomotor response to this organization.
   c) Make a locomotor response to this organization.

V. MOVEMENTS USED IN DANCE: GENERAL

Concept 1. Locomotor and nonlocomotor movements are the foundation of all dance forms.

Concept 2. Dance-like patterns and dances themselves can be created by combining various locomotor and nonlocomotor movements and making variations in space-time and force elements.

Concept 3. Qualities of movement (swinging, sustained, percussive) are utilized for expressive purposes.

Experiments

1. With rhythm instruments, produce various rhythmic patterns. Then play the following meters using even and uneven rhythmic patterns:
   a) 4/4
   b) 2/4
   c) 3/4
2. As individuals, in couples, or in groups, solve the following movement problem:

   Move for 32 counts played on a percussive instrument in moderate 4/4 time. Include three different locomotor movements and at least one non-locomotor movement. Make variations in direction, level, magnitude, and intensity.
3. Perform the locomotor and nonlocomotor movements, separately and in combination, with emphasis upon appropriate qualities (swinging, sustained, percussive).
4. In small groups, select an idea, an object, a poem, or a song upon which you will build a dance. In creating the dance, proceed as follows:
   a) Discuss the basis for the dance. Consider: characteristics; qualities, feelings, and ideas to be expressed; appropriate movements; general interpretation.
   b) Experiment with the movements.
   c) Evaluate the product in terms of intent.
   d) Refine the dance.
   e) Perform the dance for others.
   f) Again evaluate the product in terms of intent.

VI. FOLK DANCE

Concept 1. Folk dances are based upon locomotor movements, and/or combinations of locomotor movements, and usually involve variations in space-time, force.

Concept 2. Folk dance is a prestructured dance form that requires an accurate response to an imposed rhythmic pattern.

Concept 3. Proprioceptive awareness of the rhythmical organization of the movements will enable a person to continue the pattern accurately when the stimulus is removed.

Experiments

1. Perform the common folk dance steps: schottische, two-step, polka. Make variations in speed and direction.
2. Perform original dances based upon the common folk dance steps.
3. Attend to perceptual information in order to make an accurate rhythmic response.
   a) Auditory cues: listen to the accompaniment and to cue words.
   b) Visual cues: watch a demonstration of the movements.
   c) Proprioceptive cues: attend to the "feeling" of the movements.
4. As a test of proprioceptive awareness of the rhythmic organization of movements, try the following:
   a) Perform a dance, or dance steps, several times.
   b) Turn down the music until the accompaniment is not audible.
   c) Continue the dance, or dance steps, attempting to maintain the same spatial and temporal organization of movements and the intervals between movements.
   d) Near the end of the sequence, add the music again and determine whether movements and music are matched.

VII. FOLK DANCE STEPS IN SPORTS

Concept. The movement patterns that are ordinarily identified as folk dance steps are also found in sport forms.

Experiments

1. Execute a lay-up shot in basketball using the schottische step as the locomotor pattern.
   a) Is the space-time and force organization of the pattern altered when it is used for this purpose?
   b) When does the force phase of the movement occur?
   c) Which parts of the body produce great force?
   d) Which parts of the body should produce minimal force?

2. Execute a forehand drive in tennis using the two-step and pivot for positioning.
3. Guard an opponent as though you were playing basketball, using the two-step for locomotion.
   a) What other name might be applied to this movement?
   b) What advantage does this movement have over running?

VIII. GRAVITY SWING

Concept 1. A gravity swing is characterized by an initiating muscular force, a giving way to gravity, a second initiating force (muscular) as direction is changed, and another giving way to gravity.

Concept 2. The accent (force phase) of a gravity swing occurs on counts 1 and 4 when six counts are applied to the total movement.

Experiments

1. Perform a gravity swing while holding an Indian club.
   a) Hold the club in front of the body, arm extended, shoulder high.
   b) Completely relax the arm and shoulder. (Note that the club and arm fall almost straight down.)
   c) Assume the starting position again, but this time use some muscular force to guide the arm in a downward and backward direction. Use minimal muscular force, letting gravity do most of the work.
   d) As the club reaches a natural height at the end of the backswing, allow the arm to completely relax. (Note that the club and arm drop almost straight down in a jerky manner.)
   e) Perform the swing again, but this time use some muscular force to initiate the forward swing in a smooth arc.
   f) Repeat the sequence several times, noting the controlled relaxation and muscular guidance of the arm and club as gravity acts upon them. Note also that the accent (force phase) of the movement occurs on counts 1 and 4.
2. Practice the sequence in Experiment 1 with the following variations:
   a) With the eyes open.
   b) With the eyes closed.
   c) Using your preferred arm.
   d) Using your nonpreferred arm.
   e) With self-determined rhythmical organization.
   f) To a count imposed by oneself.
   g) To a count imposed by the instructor.
   h) With self-determined rhythmical organization limited by the characteristics of the gravity swing.

3. Apply the variations outlined in Experiment 2 to work with a ball. Cradle an 8½-inch ball between the hand, wrist, and forearm if real or plastic bowling balls are not available. Performers should stand about 15 feet from the wall, and roll the ball to the wall in the following manner:
   a) Feet parallel, no forward step, execute gravity swing with ankle, knee, and hip flexion as release occurs on count four. Repeat several times.
   b) The same except for addition of a forward step with the foot opposite the throwing arm as release occurs.
   c) Using the four-step approach of bowling. (Care must be taken to preserve the quality of the gravity swing.)

IX. SUSTAINED MOVEMENT

Concept. Sustained movement is characterized by constant speed.

Experiment

As you move sidewards across the floor, write your name in the air with both arms, making the movements as large and smooth as possible.

X. BALLISTIC SWING

Concept 1. A ballistic swing (as utilized in sports movements) has a sustained backswing and then forward movement is initiated by forceful muscular action.

Concept 2. The accent (force phase) of a ballistic swing occurs at the beginning of the forward swing.

Experiments

1. In partners, go through the full-speed performance of an overarm throw. One person goes through the throwing action and his partner stands on his throwing side and grabs the throwing arm just as it starts its forward movement. This is to illustrate to the thrower the power phase of the movement—the moment when vigorous exertion is essential. Try the movement several times with the eyes closed.

2. In partners, have one person throw a ball at a wall, trying to achieve as much velocity as possible. The partner should do a visual check for the following:
   a) sustained, full backswing;
   b) ballistic forward action;
   c) spinal and pelvic rotation;
   d) arm-leg opposition;
   e) complete follow-through.

3. With tennis rackets or paddles, perform the tennis serve and forehand drive with emphasis upon the sustained "wind-up" and ballistic forward action. Diagram or notate the rhythmic organization of these two movements.

4. Combine the two-step and pivot with the forehand drive. Emphasis should be upon the coordination of all movements while preserving the unique rhythmic organization of each.

XI. ANALYSIS OF RHYTHMIC ORGANIZATION

Concept. All movements can be analyzed in terms of their rhythmic organization—their quality or combination of qualities.

Experiment

Analyze and diagram or notate the rhythmic organization of the various movement patterns listed below.
   a) Sport movement patterns
   b) Gymnastic movement patterns
   c) Aquatic movement patterns
   d) Dance movement patterns

XII. EFFICIENCY AND RHYTHMIC ORGANIZATION

Concept. Movements can become more efficient and more consistent if attention is given to their rhythmic organization.

Experiments

1. Practice one or more of the movement patterns analyzed in the preceding experiment.
   a) Increase efficiency by application of all movement principles. Focus especially upon the rhythmic organization of the movement.
   b) Develop consistency by the recognition and reproduction of the rhythmic organization on successive occasions.

appendix I
A MINIMAL GENERAL CONDITIONING PROGRAM

The general conditioning program described here will help you develop cardio-vascular-respiratory endurance and selected aspects of strength and flexibility through a brief but systematically arranged period of exercise performed at least three times per week. The program is designed to meet the minimum needs of most individuals in relation to some of the demands of sport, dance, aquatic, and daily-life activities. A suggested 16-week progression for the seven exercises that are described is given in Chart A–1. Additional exercises may be assigned by your instructor.

Note that this program is both *minimal* and *general*. It does not include exercises specifically designed to improve your performance in any given sport, nor does it focus on such special objectives as relaxation or posture improvement. In Chapter 10 you will find a great deal of information to help you in tailoring a personal exercise program to those needs. What the program outlined here will do is help keep you fit enough to engage in a normal amount of vigorous physical activity without undue strain.

Some instructors will choose to use this exercise program, or modifications of it, as a regular opening activity of each class, in preparation for any other activity scheduled. Whether or not this is the case, there is every good reason for you to incorporate the program in your out-of-class routine. It is so brief and simple that no one can truthfully claim lack of time as an excuse for rejecting it—and the rewards are great in proportion to the time expended.

The most obvious of these rewards is simply the improvement you can make in each of the selected components of physical fitness listed at the beginning of the exercises. It is hoped that your instructor will help you measure that improvement by testing you before you embark on the 16-week progression and after you have completed it. The nature of such testing and its scoring will depend, of course, on what equipment and measuring devices are available. A form for recording pretest and posttest scores is given in

Chart A–2. Two worksheets, Appendixes II and III, can be used for keeping a record of your improvement.

Selected components of physical fitness

1. Push arm strength
2. Pull arm strength
3. Finger grip strength
4. Abdominal muscle strength and flexibility
5. Lower back and hamstring strength and flexibility
6. Lateral trunk muscle strength and flexibility
7. Cardiovascular-respiratory endurance

Exercise principles

1. *Strength development:* The overload principle is utilized in isometric exercises by a gradual increase in the level of maximum contraction.
2. *Development of flexibility:* Gravity is utilized as the force to increase joint mobility in selected regions of the body.
3. *Development of cardiovascular-respiratory endurance:* An exercise involving total body action with provision for a gradual increase in the total number of repetitions is intended to develop cardiovascular-respiratory endurance.

Exercise	Purpose	Description
1. Isometric push Push	To strengthen the arm and shoulder, horizontal adductors.	Abduct arms from the body, flex at elbows, bring palms together. With elbows at shoulder height and pointed away from the body, push the palms together as hard as possible, and then relax.*

* No specified amount of time for holding a contraction is given. Recent information indicates that individuals do not achieve a maximum contraction if they attempt to *hold* the contraction over a given period of time.

Exercise	Purpose	Description
2. Isometric pull  Pull	To strengthen the arm and shoulder, horizontal abductors.	Abduct arms from the body, flex at elbows, flex the fingers, and lock finger tips. With hands locked, pull arms away from each other as hard as possible, and then relax.*
3. Isometric grip 	To strengthen the hand and finger flexors.	Grasp the left wrist with right hand, squeeze as hard as possible by flexing fingers in grasping motion, and then relax. Alternate by grasping right wrist with left hand and squeezing as hard as possible, then relax.*
4. Abdominal isometric 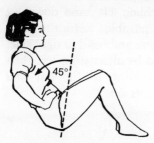 45°	To strengthen the abdominal muscles.	Start in a sitting position, hands on hips, knees flexed, and feet flat on the floor. Gradually lower the body to a 45° angle and hold the position for approximately six seconds.

* No specified amount of time for holding a contraction is given. Recent information indicates that individuals do not achieve a maximum contraction if they attempt to *hold* the contraction over a given period of time.

Exercise	Purpose	Description
5. Toe touching	To stretch and strengthen the lower back and hamstring muscles.	Stand erect, feet 12 inches apart, arms over head. Slowly bend forward as far as possible to touch floor between feet. Keep the knees straight. Return to the starting position. Each return to the starting position counts one.

| 6. Lateral trunk strength and flexibility | To stretch and strengthen the lateral trunk muscles. | Stand erect, feet 12 inches apart, hands at sides. Avoid inclining trunk forward or backward and slowly bend sidewards from waist to left. Slide left hand down leg as far as possible. Return to starting position and bend to right side. Continue by alternating left then right. Bending to the left *and* right counts *one*. |

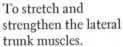

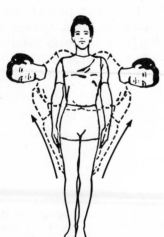

Exercise	Purpose	Description

7. Running and jumping

To develop cardiovascular-respiratory endurance.

Stand erect, feet together, arms at sides. Starting with left leg, run in place, raising feet at least four inches from floor. (When running in place, lift knees forward, do not merely kick heels backward.) Each time the left foot touches the floor counts one. After each fifty counts do ten jumps in place. Try to jump at least four inches off the floor each time. *Note:* In all run-in-place exercises, only *running* steps are counted toward completing exercise repetitions.

CHART A-1   Exercise Progression

Week	Exercise Number						
	1	2	3	4	5	6	7
	Duration				Number of Repetitions		
1	6 sec.	6 sec.	6 sec.	6 sec.	3	5	60
2	"	"	"	"	5	7	70
3	"	"	"	"	7	9	80
4	"	"	"	"	9	11	100
5	"	"	"	"	10	13	120
6	"	"	"	"	12	15	140
7	"	"	"	"	14	17	160
8	"	"	"	"	16	19	170
9	"	"	"	"	18	21	180
10	"	"	"	"	20	23	190
11 to 16	"	"	"	"	20	25	200

CHART A-2   Form for Recording Selected Fitness Test Scores

Item	Pretest Score	Posttest Score
1. Push strength		
2. Pull strength		
3. Grip strength		
4. Abdominal muscle strength and flexibility		
5. Lower back and hamstring strength and flexibility		
6. Lateral trunk muscle strength and flexibility		
7. Cardiovascular-respiratory endurance		

Additional

8.		
9.		
10.		

WORKSHEET FOR RECORDING BODY PROPORTIONS

Body area and ideal measurements	Actual Measurements				Exercises
	Date	Date	Date	Date	
Bust					
Waist					
Abdomen					
Hips					
Thigh					
Calf					
Ankle					

appendix III

WORKSHEET FOR SELF-ASSESSMENT

Capabilities before program	Acquired or projected capabilities

GLOSSARY

Abilities: General traits or characteristics of an individual such as reaction time or movement time.

Accent (as a compositional element):   An object or event that is distinguishable from other objects or events because of the distinctive stress placed on it.

Aesthetic Criteria: Those devices for measurement or evaluation by which one assesses the relative position, aesthetically, of a unique, creative, human expression.

Affectors: Factors that influence and/or initiate responses.

Afferents: Nerves that transmit information sent by receptors.

Alveoli: Air sacs of the lungs.

Arteries: Vessels that carry blood away from the heart.

Art Form: A vehicle used by an individual to express an idea or feeling. Some examples of art forms are sculpture, painting, music, and dance.

Balance (as a compositional element):   General harmony between objects and events and equilibrium achieved by symmetry or asymmetry.

Bipedalism: Locomotion on two feet.

Bone: The hardest of all connective tissue, composing most of the skeletal structure of the adult human.

Calorie: The amount of heat required to raise the temperature of one kilogram of water one degree centigrade.

Cardiac Output: The product of the heart rate and the stroke volume.

Cardiovascular: A term referring to both the heart (cardio) and the blood vessels (vascular) of the circulatory system.

Collagenous Fibers: Strong, inelastic tissue of the body.

183

Color (as a compositional element): The quality or characteristic of an object or event that excites emotional response in the viewer or listener. In painting this is achieved by conscious arrangement of hues, tints, and shades of pigment. In dance, color often is imparted by leaps and turns and movements that have a vertiginous quality. A "colorful" basketball player is one who employs a great variety of movement sequences and skills during the game.

Concentric Contraction: Contraction in which, as a muscle shortens, the body segment is displaced in the direction of the muscle's line of pull.

Contraction: The action by which a muscle becomes shorter. This process involves the interaction between the two types of filaments of which fibrils are composed. (See also Muscle Fibers.)

Contrast (as a compositional element): The heightened perceptual effect achieved by placing next to each other two objects or events with opposite qualities or characteristics.

Eccentric Contraction: The gradual release of tension in a muscle as it gives in to gravity or a force greater than that of the contracting muscle.

Effectors: Those agents that perform or facilitate a response, such as muscles or glands.

Efferents: Nerves that transmit messages that activate muscles.

Elastic Fibers: Tissues of the body that possess the quality of resiliency; they are thinner than collagenous fibers.

Endurance: The ability to maintain a submaximal rate of muscular work over relatively extended periods of time without undue fatigue.

Erythrocytes: Red cells of the blood.

Experiential: An adjective describing a quality or characteristic that has been developed through, or derived from, observation or experience.

Exteroceptors: End organs of the receptors located at or near the body's surface, which respond to conditions in the external environment.

Feedback: Information from the receptors during the execution of a movement response, and information from the receptors concerning the outcomes effected by that response.

Frontal Plane: A plane that divides the body into a front and back portion.

Fulcrum: The point at which a lever pivots.

Gross Motor Skill: A series of movement sequences that require the dynamic involvement of the large muscles of the body as well as the small ones. In general, the performance of such a skill moves the entire body through space. An example of a gross motor skill is the basketball jump shot, as opposed to the fine motor skill of writing a sentence on a piece of paper while seated at a desk.

Heart Rate: Frequency of heart beats per unit of time.

Hemoglobin: Material in red cells of the blood that readily takes up oxygen.

Input: Pertinent physical stimuli that are actually "sensed" by the individual prior to response.

Isometric: An adjective meaning "of equal measure," used as a synonym for static contraction when muscle tension is maximum.

Isotonic: An adjective meaning "of equal tension," a commonly used synonym for concentric contraction.

Interoceptors: Receptors housed in the internal areas of the body that send information to the central nervous system concerning conditions of the internal environment, e.g., pain, hunger, and thirst.

Joint: Union of one bone with another.

Lever: A rigid bar which turns about a fixed point called a fulcrum.

Leukocytes: White cells of the blood.

Line (as a compositional element):   A conscious plan of action, direction, and/or construction calculated to stimulate specific perceptual experiences in the listener to or viewer of a work of art.

Ligaments: Tissues that unite bone to bone; most are formed of collagenous-type fibers, though a few are almost entirely composed of elastic fibers.

Metabolism: The process of converting foodstuffs into the energy which drives biological reactions.

Modality (sense):   The vehicle or manner by which stimuli are transferred over the central nervous system, e.g., vision is a sense modality.

Mode: A prevailing practice or custom, manner or style.

Motor End Plate: The termination of a branch of an axon (part of a neuron), which is in contact with the surface of a single muscle fiber.

Motor Fibers: Nerve tissues that conduct impulses from the central nervous system to the muscles.

Motor Task: Any specified amount of work or a performance that demands voluntary movement.

Motor Unit: A motor neuron and all the muscle fibers that the neuron serves.

Movement Behavior: An individual's unique and characteristic manner of moving the body and/or body segments in space and time.

Movement Form: Every organized and purposeful collection or constellation of movement sequences which have rules and/or conventions as well as a recognizable structure. To participate one must conform to the limitations imposed by these rules and/or conventions of the form itself, whether it is basketball, tap dance, or synchronized swimming.

Movement Sequence: Any set of actions that are structured without orientation to a specific movement form, e.g., running, walking, throwing, striking, kicking.

Movement Skill: See Skill.

Muscle: Contractile tissue of the body.

Muscle Fibers: Strands of muscle tissue, each one bounded by connective tissue and consisting of many bundles of closely packed fibrils. These strands form the skeletal muscles.

Neuron: The basic unit of the nervous system composed of a cell body, dendrites, and an axon.

Optical Illusions: Deceptive or faulty perceptions of the shape, magnitude, color, position, and/or motion of a visually sensed object or event.

Output: The observable responses of an individual to an object or event.

Overload: A term used to describe the process, in exercise, of gradually increasing either the resistance against which a muscle works, or the number of times a muscle works against an amount of resistance that is held constant. This process should occur over successive bouts of exercise.

Perceiving: The conscious act of recognition or "knowing."

Perception: A coding and organizing process that is an intermediate stage between reception of stimuli and movement responses.

Perceptual-Motor Coordination: The cyclic, complex interrelationship consisting of the organization of sensory and nonsensory data into perceptions that guide the human organism in producing efficient, voluntary movement behavior.

Periosteum: Dense fibrous tissue covering the bones.

Physiological Fitness: A term used to describe the relative efficiency with which an individual performs muscular work over a given period of time.

Plateaus (in learning or performance):   Intervals during which responses of an individual seem to remain at the same level of proficiency without observable retrogression or improvement—a *status quo* situation.

Pressure Receptors: Sense organs that receive and transmit information about the varying degrees of pressure exerted on the skin and viscera. These receptors are the Pacinian corpuscles, which are found in the skin below the tactile receptors as well as in the lining of the visceral cavity.

Proprioceptors: Receptors found in the muscles, tendons, joints, and labyrinth of the inner ear that provide information about the locations and positions of the body and body segments in space.

Pulmonary System: That portion of the circulatory system which moves non-oxygenated blood from the right side of the heart to the lungs and oxygenated blood from the lungs back to the left side of the heart.

Quadruped: An animal that uses four legs for locomotion.

Receptors: Structures in the sense organs that are sensitive to stimulation.

Repetition (as a compositional element):   The recurrence of an object or event.

Respiration: The exchange of oxygen and carbon dioxide between the cells of the body and the outside environment.

Response Modification: The process by which the rhythmic structure, speed, and direction of movement sequences are adjusted by the performer during repeated trials. Thus the subsequent responses should more nearly approach the efficiency and accuracy potentials of that individual.

Rhythm (as a compositional element): A systematic grouping of objects or events and a regulated arrangement of such groups. It is movement that is characterized by a regulated succession of different or opposite conditions.

Sagittal Plane: A plane that divides the body into a right portion and a left portion.

Scintillation Counter: See Whole-Body Liquid Scintillation Counter.

Sensation: The transformed energy of a stimulus that travels over the receptors and afferent nerves of the central nervous system.

Sensory Feedback: See also Feedback. *Concurrent*—sensations arising from stimuli produced during the execution of a movement sequence or skill. *Terminal* —sensations arising from stimuli produced as a result of the completed movement or skill, e.g., the distance the golf ball traveled or the direction in which the baseball went after being hit.

Sensory Fibers: Nerve tissues that carry impulses from both the exterior and interior of the body to the central nervous system.

Skill: A specific combination of movement sequences such as occurs in a basketball jump shot, a figure-eight in ice-skating, or tying a shoe.

Skillfulness: The level of proficiency with which one performs a skill.

Slow Stretch: The gradual increasing of the length of the elastic tissues, which tie the joints of the body together, beyond their resting length and slightly beyond the initial stage of discomfort.

Socio-Cultural: The total differential influence of all environmental objects in the individual's perceptual field.

Space (as a compositional element): An area that is bounded by lines, or denoted by the absence, presence, or difference of color. Space may also be the interval between objects or events. It may be two-dimensional as in painting or three-dimensional as in sculpture. In dance, space is four-dimensional because the element of time is present as well as height, width, and depth.

Static Contraction: The partial or complete contraction of a muscle with no apparent displacement of body segments.

Stimuli: Changes in the physical energy of some aspect of the internal and/or external environment.

Stroke Volume: Amount of blood ejected by the heart per beat.

Sudden Stretch: The abrupt increase in the length of the elastic tissues, which tie the joints of the body together, beyond their resting length and slightly beyond the initial stage of discomfort. It is usually accomplished by ballistic movement such as "bobbing" (not recommended).

Systemic System: That portion of the circulatory system which moves blood to and from tissues of the body not served by the pulmonary system.

Tactile Receptors: Sense organs housed in the skin and sensitive to touch. There are three types of tactile receptors; one type is twined around the base of hair follicles and the other two (Meissner's corpuscles and Merkel's discs) are found in great abundance in the hairless skin areas such as the palms of the hands and soles of the feet.

Tendons: Tissues that connect muscles to bones and are formed primarily of collagenous-type fibers.

Transverse Plane: A plane which divides the body into an upper portion and a lower portion.

Veins: Vessels which carry blood to the heart.

Velocity: A quantity which describes the speed and direction of an object.

Whole-Body Liquid Scintillation Counter: An instrument that measures gamma rays emitted by potassium in the body.

BIBLIOGRAPHY

Note: The boldface number in parentheses at the end of each reference indicates the chapter to which the cited reference is applicable.

Andrews, Gladys, *Creative Rhythmic Movement for Children*. Englewood Cliffs, N.J.: Prentice-Hall, Inc., 1954. (**4**)

Bigge, Morris L., *Learning Theories for Teachers*. New York: Harper and Row, Publishers, 1964. (**7**)

Bruner, Jerome S., *On Knowing*. New York: Atheneum, 1965. (**5**)

Bruner, Jerome S., *et al.*, *Studies in Cognitive Growth*. New York: John Wiley and Sons, Inc., 1966. (**5**)

Clark, Margaret and Margaret Lantis, "Sports in a changing culture," *Journal of Health, Physical Education and Recreation* 29, 37–39. (**4**)

Cofer, Charles N. and Mortimer H. Appley, *Motivation: Theory and Research*. New York: John Wiley and Sons, Inc., 1967. (**1**)

DeLorme, Thomas L. and A. L. Watkins, *Progressive Resistance Exercise: Technique and Medical Application*. New York: Appleton-Century-Crofts, Inc., 1951. (**8**)

Dember, William N., *Psychology of Perception*. New York: Holt, Rinehart and Winston, 1963. (**5**)

Farber, Seymour M. and Roger H. L. Wilson (eds.), *Conflict and Creativity*. New York: McGraw-Hill Book Company, Inc., 1963. (**6**)

Fitts, Paul M. and Michael I. Posner, *Human Performance*. Belmont, Calif.: Brooks/Cole Publishing Company, 1967. (**7**)

Frederickson, Florence S., "Sport and the culture of man," in *Science and Medicine of Exercise and Sports*, Warren R. Johnson (ed.). New York: Harper and Row, Publishers, 1960. (**4**)

Gagné, Robert M., *The Conditions of Learning*. New York: Holt, Rinehart and Winston, Inc., 1965. (**7**)

H'Doubler, Margaret, *Movement and Its Rhythmic Structure*. Madison, Wisc.: Kramer Business Service, 1946. (**12**)

Hebb, D. O., *Organization of Behavior*. New York: John Wiley and Sons, 1964. (5)

Hellebrandt, F. A., "Application of the overload principle to muscle training in man," *American Journal of Physical Medicine* 37, 278–283 (1958). (8)

Hubbard, Alfred W., "Homokinetics: muscular function in human movement," in *Science and Medicine of Exercise and Sports*, Warren R. Johnson (ed.). New York: Harper and Row, Publishers, 1960. (12)

Jokl, Ernst, "Sport as leisure," *Quest*, **Mono. IV**, 37–46. (4)

———, *Medical Sociology and Cultural Anthropology of Sport and Physical Education*. Springfield, Ill.: Charles C. Thomas, 1964. (4)

Kimble, Gregory A., *Hilgard and Marquis' Conditioning and Learning*. New York: Appleton-Century-Crofts, Inc., 1961. (7)

Klausmeier, Herbert J. and William Goodwin, *Learning and Human Abilities*. New York: Harper and Row, Publishers, 1966. (7)

Kraus, Hans and Wilhelm Raab, *Hypokinetic Disease*. Springfield, Ill.: Charles C. Thomas, 1961. (8)

Laban, Rudolph, *The Mastery of Movement*. London: MacDonald and Evans, 1960. (1)

Laban, Rudolph and F. C. Lawrence, *Effort*. London: MacDonald and Evans, 1947. (1)

Langer, Susanne K., *Problems of Art*. New York: Charles Scribner's Sons, 1957. (6)

Leibowitz, Herschel W., *Visual Perception*. New York: The Macmillan Company, 1965. (5)

McIntosh, Peter E., *Sport in Society*. London: C. A. Watts, 1963. (4)

McPhee, John, *A Sense of Where You Are*. New York: Bantam Books, Inc., 1965. (5)

Mednick, Sarnoff A., *Learning*. Englewood Cliffs, N.J.: Prentice-Hall, Inc., 1964. (7)

Metheny, Eleanor, *Body Dynamics*. New York: McGraw-Hill Book Company, Inc., 1952. (9)

———, *Connotations of Movement in Sport and Dance*. Dubuque, Iowa: Wm. C. Brown Co., 1965. (4)

Michotte, A., *The Perception of Causality*. New York: Basic Books, Inc., 1963. (5)

Mosscrop, Alfreda, Helen Hardenbergh, and Grace M. Rockwood, *Apparatus Activity for Girls*. Minneapolis, Minn.: Burgess Publishing Company, 1952. (11)

Mosston, Muska, *Developmental Movement*. Columbus, Ohio: Charles E. Merrill Books, Inc., 1965. (1)

Muller, E. A., "The regulation of muscle strength," *Journal of the Association for Physical and Mental Rehabilitation* 11, 41–47 (1957). (8)

Piaget, Jean, *The Origins of Intelligence in Children*. New York: International Universities Press, Inc., 1952. (5)

Provaznik, Marie and Norma Zabka, *Gymnastic Activities with Hand Apparatus*. Minneapolis, Minn.: Burgess Publishing Company, 1965. (11)

Ragsdale, Clarence E., *The Psychology of Motor Learning*. Ann Arbor, Mich.: Edwards Brothers, 1930. (7)

Randall, Marjorie, *Basic Movement—A New Approach to Gymnastics*. London: G. L. and Sons, Limited, 1961. (11)

Roberts, John M., *et al.*, "Games in culture," *American Anthropologist* 61, 597–605. (4)

Ruch, Theodore C. and Harry D. Patton, *Physiology and Biophysics*. Philadelphia: W. B. Saunders Company, 1965. (2)

Smith, Karl and William Smith, *Perception and Motion*. Philadelphia: W. B. Saunders Company, 1962. (5)

Smith, MacFarlane, *Spatial Ability*. San Diego, Calif.: Robert R. Knapp, 1964. (5)

Solomon, Philip, *et al.* (eds.), *Sensory Deprivation*. Cambridge, Mass.: Harvard University Press, 1961. (5)

Spigel, Irwin M., *Readings in the Study of Visually Perceived Movement*. New York: Harper and Row, Publishers, 1965. (5)

Stein, Morris I. and Shirley J. Heinze, *Creativity and the Individual*. Glencoe, Ill.: The Free Press, 1960. (6)

Sutton-Smith, Brian, *et al.*, "Game involvement in adults," *Journal of Social Psychology* 15, 60. (4)

Symonds, Percival M., *What Education Has to Learn from Psychology*. New York: Teachers College Press, Columbia University, 1960. (7)

Tricker, R. A. R. and B. J. K. Tricker, *The Science of Movement*. New York: American Elsevier Publishing Co., Inc., 1967. (3)

Wessel, Janet A., *Movement Fundamentals—Figure, Form, Fun*, second edition. Englewood Cliffs, N.J., Prentice-Hall, Inc., 1961. (9)

Wolfe, C., *A Psychology of Gesture*. London: Methuen and Company, 1945. (4)

Woodburne, Lloyd S., *The Neural Basis of Behavior*. Columbus, Ohio: Charles E. Merrill Book, Inc., 1967. (5)

Woody, Thomas, *Life and Education in Early Societies*. New York: The Macmillan Company, 1949. (4)

INDEX